Publications of the

CENTRE FOR REFORMATION AND RENAISSANCE STUDIES

Renaissance and Reformation Texts in Translation, 1

SERIES EDITOR   John McClelland

Victoria University

in the

University of Toronto

The Profession
of the Religious

and selections from

The Falsely-Believed and
Forged Donation of
Constantine

Lorenzo Valla

Translated, with an Introduction and Notes, by
Olga Zorzi Pugliese

3rd Edition, Revised

Toronto
Centre for Reformation and Renaissance Studies
1998

CRRS Publications
Centre for Reformation and Renaissance Studies
Victoria University in the University of Toronto
Toronto, Canada M5S 1K7

Canadian Cataloguing in Publication Data

Valla, Lorenzo, 1406–1457
  The profession of the religious and selections
from The falsely–believed and forged donation of
Constantine

(Renaissance and Reformation texts in translation ; 1)
2nd ed. rev. & aug.
Translation of: De professione religiosorum and De
falso credita et ementita Constantini donatione.
Includes bibliographical references.
ISBN 0–9697512–3–0

1. Monastic and religious life – Controversial
literature – Early works to 1800. 2. Constitutum
Constantini. 3. Popes – Temporal power –
Controversial literature – Early works to 1800.
I. Pugliese, Olga Zorzi, 1941–   . II. Victoria
University (Toronto, Ont.). Centre for Reformation
and Renaissance Studies. III. Title. IV. Series.

BX 2439.A2V35   1994   255   C94–932876 66

Cover illustration: Lorenzo Valla, engraved by Theodor de Bry (*c.* 1597), in
Bibliotheca Chalcographica (Heidelberg, 1669).

Contents

Introduction

Lorenzo Valla and His Works

The Profession of the Religious and *The Falsely-Believed and Forged Donation of Constantine* were written by Lorenzo Valla (1407–57), one of the chief fashioners of Italian humanism in the fifteenth century. They illustrate many aspects of Renaissance culture: the revival of learning, the development of humanist philology, the masterly way in which Renaissance authors adapted classical rhetoric, as well as their concern for ethical matters treated above all from the point of view of human experience.[1] Furthermore, these works occupy an important position in the history of the religious thought of the period.[2] A bold thinker, Valla aroused controversy in his own circles in Italy when his writings first appeared. Posthumously too, he exerted considerable influence especially on Protestant reformers of the following century. *The Donation* (1440), his most notorious treatise, was first edited in Germany, Switzerland, France, and England early in the 1500s and by mid-century it had been translated into the vernacular languages, including French, German, English, and Italian.[3] A particularly successful edition was

---

[1] For the standard treatment of these aspects of the Renaissance, see Eugenio Garin, *Italian Humanism: Philosophy and Civic Life in the Renaissance*, trans. Peter Munz (Oxford: Basil Blackwell, 1965); and Paul Oskar Kristeller, *Renaissance Thought and Its Sources* (New York: Columbia UP, 1979).

[2] A comprehensive view of the religious thought of the period is provided in Donald J. Wilcox, *In Search of God and Self: Renaissance and Reformation Thought* (Boston: Houghton Mifflin, 1975).

[3] For details on the numerous editions see the introduction to the edition by

that of 1518 and 1519 prepared by the reformer Ulrich von Hutten, who prefaced Valla's text with an ironical dedication to Pope Leo X. Martin Luther was one of those who identified with the antipapal stand taken by Valla. In a letter dated February 24, 1520, he credited Valla's work with having revealed to him the evils of the Church of Rome.[4] *The Profession* (c. 1440), on the other hand, circulated in manuscript form only and, although it was mentioned by the Lutheran reformer Matthias Flacius Illyricus,[5] for example, the treatise was not so well known. The Latin original was not published until last century, a complete Italian version appeared in 1953, and the first English translation to date is the present one. Had the treatise been more readily available during the Reformation, it too, undoubtedly, like *The Donation,* would have contributed more substantially to its author's fame.

Born in Rome in 1407, Valla spent his youth studying the classics both independently (at times through contacts in the Papal Curia where members of his family held posts) and also with eminent masters of Greek and Latin.[6] He moved to Northern Italy and was made professor of rhetoric at the University of Pavia in 1431. Forced to leave just two years later when he became embroiled in one of his frequent polemics—this time after having attacked the work of Bartolo da Sassoferrato (d. 1357), a leading mediaeval writer on civil law, for his failure to understand ancient Roman jurisprudence—he eventually headed South again, visiting several cities including Florence on the way. Unable to secure the position in the Curia he so ardently desired, Valla accepted appointment as secretary to the king of Naples, Alfonso V of Aragon. As the monarch's counsellor and historian, he spent the period from 1435 to 1448 accompanying Alfonso even on his military campaigns and distinguished himself as the most eminent member of the literary circle in the king's court

---

Setz, and pp. 189–92 in Antonazzi's study listed in the Select Bibliography.

[4] *Luther's Correspondence and Other Contemporary Letters*, trans. and ed. Preserved Smith (Philadelphia: Lutheran Publication Society, 1913), 1:290–91.

[5] A quotation from the reformer's writings indicating his knowledge of Valla's work is cited in Agostino Sottili, "Notizie sul 'Nachleben' di Valla tra Umanesimo e Riforma," in *Lorenzo Valla e l'Umanesimo italiano: atti del convegno internazionale di studi umanistici* (Padua: Antenore, 1986), 342.

[6] For Valla's life, see the studies by Mancini and Barozzi-Sabbadini listed in the Select Bibliography.

in Naples. In recognition for his service, the king conferred upon Valla, who had not attended university, academic titles in the liberal arts and in civil and canon law. As for his clerical status, it seems Valla took minor orders in the Catholic Church and received some ecclesiastical benefices, but did not enter the priesthood. In his last years he served as a canon of St. John Lateran in Rome. Although he did not marry, he had three children by his sister's house-keeper—a situation which earned him many personal attacks from his adversaries.

It was during his stay in Gaeta near Naples that Valla composed *The Profession* and *The Donation*. Companion pieces, dating prob-ably from the same year 1440,[7] they exhibit a powerful criticism of ecclesiastical instititutions. In the first the author takes to task the members of religious orders for their claims to superiority because of their vows. In the second he questions the legal and historical grounds for the papacy's increasing temporal activities. The fierce-ness of Valla's criticism, especially pronounced in *The Donation*, may be related to his dependence on King Alfonso who was, until 1443, a bitter enemy of Pope Eugenius IV.[8] Alfonso was struggling at the time to consolidate control over Naples, while the pope, ruler of one of the major powers in the Italian peninsula, favoured a rival Anjou contender. The king, in turn, lent his support to the Council of Basel that was challenging the supreme authority of the Roman Pontiff. His action was obviously not an unadulterated commitment to the conciliar movement, but rather a means of undermining Eugenius who stood in the way of his political ambitions.

---

[7] This dating of *The Profession* has been argued convincingly by Monfasani in his review article listed in the Select Bibliography. He rejects Cortesi's hypothesis for the place and date of composition—Benevento 1440—in favour of Gaeta, January 1440. The dating of *The Donation*, on the other hand, has always been based on a reference made in the text (XXVIII, 91) to a rebellion against the pope that had occurred six years earlier.

[8] On the political situation of the time see Jerry H. Bentley, *Politics and Culture in Renaissance Naples* (Princeton, NJ: Princeton UP, 1987); Alan Ryder, *Alfonso the Magnanimous King of Aragon, Naples and Sicily, 1396-1458* (Oxford: Clarendon, 1990); and Joachim W. Stieber, *Pope Eugenius IV, the Council of Basel and the Secular and Ecclesiastical Authorities in the Empire: The Conflict over Supreme Authority and Power in the Church* (Leiden: Brill, 1978).

A conspiracy, organized in all likelihood by papal sympathizers, is mentioned in *The Profession*. Although it may not correspond exactly to any specific event recorded for that era, since even the data examined by Mariarosa Cortesi in her recent critical edition of the text does not appear to solve the mystery,[9] it does indicate the turbulence of the environment in which Valla was forced to live. Alfonso's feud with the pope came to an end after the king achieved his political conquest of Naples in 1442 and signed a pact with the pontiff in 1443. Yet Valla still faced danger because of the unconventional views he had expressed in his treatises. He was questioned by the Inquisition in Naples and was threatened with another inquiry for heresy in Rome when he went there briefly in 1444. It was apparently only through the king's intercession that he was saved.

Valla made repeated requests to return permanently to his native Rome but, not surprisingly, because of his attack on the papacy, especially in his work on the donation, in which he accuses Eugenius IV of cowardice and incompetence (XXVIII, 91), the pope left his pleas unanswered. In 1444 Valla addressed an *Apology* to Eugenius IV. In it he defends himself and insists that he has been accused unjustly by envious rivals (and these were numerous in humanist circles). He offers no compliant retraction, though; consistently defending his actions and his writings, including *The Profession*, he states that his religious faith is unshaken and that it conforms to orthodox Catholicism. Valla always considered himself a "soldier" fighting for his religion (*The Profession*, X) and viewed his activities (including those of a literary nature) as battles directed against error and corruption for the sake of "truth," "justice," and "God," as he proclaims at the beginning of the oration on the donation of Constantine (I, 2). In a letter to Cardinal Ludovico Trevisan (November 19, 1443) written to appeal his ban from Rome, he states that he had been forced to compose the work—a statement that might lend credence to existing interpretations of the two texts as mere Aragonese propaganda;[10] however, in the same letter he

---

[9] According to Monfasani, the research carried out so far has not led to a satisfactory identification of the conspiracy alluded to in the text.

[10] See Fois on *The Donation* and Guidi, "Lorenzo Valla," on *The Profession* (both studies are included in the Select Bibliography).

adds that he wrote the treatise in defence of truth and the faith, not out of personal hatred toward the Pope.[11] Eugenius was not to be swayed, though, and it was only after his death in 1447 that his successors ultimately decided to employ Valla's talents for their own benefit. Nicholas V engaged him in 1448 as letter writer and Callixtus III finally fulfilled Valla's overriding ambition, by naming him Apostolic Secretary in 1455, to the dismay of such rival scholars as Poggio Bracciolini.

Valla did not have to wait so long to gain recognition in the educational field. He had taught at the University of Pavia early in his career and, while in Naples and in Rome, he regularly gave private lessons in classical studies. During the last seven years of his life, he occupied the chair of rhetoric at the University of Rome which, after a long interruption, had been opened again.

A devoted student of antiquity, Valla read manuscripts of the classics avidly and translated works by Homer, Aesop, Herodotus, Thucydides, and others. It is from these scholarly pursuits that much of his own literary production stems. His earliest work, dating from 1428 and now lost, consisted of a comparison between the Roman orators Cicero and Quintilian in which, contrary to general humanist thinking, Valla indicated his preference for Quintilian's art of rhetoric. His claim to have actually memorized Quintilian is borne out by the frequent use he made of the orator's precepts in his own writings.[12] The relation between rhetoric and philosophy is the subject of *Disputations on Dialectics* (1439) in which the methods of oratory are hailed as being closer to human experience than those of metaphysics and dialectic used by mediaeval scholastic philosophers. The rhetorical method, Valla argues, is more valid since it is based on probability and makes use of ordinary language rather than abstract terminology or sophistic distinctions. In his history of King Ferdinand of Aragon, composed in 1445, Valla demonstrates the same inclination toward the concrete when he proclaims historians superior to philosophers. He warns against the dangers of philosophical systems in his treatise on *The True Good*, the earliest version of which, completed in 1431, was entitled *On Pleasure*. This

---

[11] Valla, *Epistole* (edition cited in the Select Bibliography), 247–48.

[12] He makes this claim in his invective against Bartolomeo Facio (see *Opera*, listed in the Select Bibliography, 1:477).

dialogue between a defender of Stoicism, an advocate of Epicureanism, and a Christian concludes with the victory of the last. Its
compromise solution, a form of Christian Epicureanism, allows man
to lead a full life on earth and then to achieve happiness in heaven.

In his treatise *On Free Will* begun in 1435, Valla questions the
usefulness of philosophy in debating not only ethical problems but
theological ones as well. Opposed to attempts made by scholastic
philosophers like Boethius to reconcile faith and reason, Valla
maintains that theological matters are open questions. Mankind
must rely on faith alone, and love God, as Saint Paul teaches, rather
than try to understand Him intellectually. This statement was to find
favour among the Protestants. Luther, for example, thought that
Valla was on his side and had anticipated the idea of justification by
faith.[13] Actually, however, Valla expresses a moderate Catholic concept which aims at harmonizing divine grace with the human will.

Another religious thinker attracted to Valla's writings was Erasmus of Rotterdam (d. 1536).[14] As a young man he prepared abridged
versions of Valla's *The Elegance of the Latin Language* (1441–48), a
treatise on correct Latin usage meant to supersede the faulty gram-
mars produced in the Middle Ages. Valla's text, which became the
standard manual on Latin, was first published in 1471 and ran
through approximately sixty editions in the Renaissance alone.
Clearly his most successful composition, the work contains notions
of language as based on usage: for Valla, grammar is the basis of all
knowledge—of philosophy, law, and even theology; the Latin language in particular is "sacramental" since it enabled the Romans to
spread their highly evolved civilization to many peoples. A similar
view on the importance of language is expressed in a brief versified
Art of Grammar (1442–43) that has been attributed to Valla. It states
that "all disciplines need grammar, but grammar needs no other, and
those who are ignorant of this art feed on polenta mush" (vv. 21–22).

Valla applied his knowledge of language to the Bible too. In his
Annotations to the New Testament (1442–57) he carefully collated

---

[13] Martin Luther, *The Bondage of the Will*, trans. Philip S. Watson in
collaboration with Benjamin Drewery, *Luther's Works* (Philadelphia: Fortress
Press, 1972), vol. 33 of 72.

[14] R.J. Schoeck, "Erasmus and Valla: The Dynamics of a Relationship,"
Erasmus of Rotterdam Society Yearbook 12 (1992), 45–63.

Greek and Latin versions of the New Testament and thus was able to elucidate passages in the Vulgate that did not convey accurately enough the sense of the Greek text. This pacemaking contribution made by the Italian humanist to biblical philology was published for the first time in 1505 by Erasmus, who subsequently carried out this type of exegetical research even further himself.

The philological and rhetorical emphasis on precise and effective language and the scorn for metaphysical subtleties, expressed in a number of Valla's writings, are essential aspects of the methodology on which the treatises on the profession of the religious and on the donation of Constantine are founded. Like the author's other works these are written in Latin and polemically challenge established authorities; they reflect Valla's consistent indictment of scholastic culture in favour of a Pauline type of religion based on charity; and they advocate the inner spirituality and eloquent style characteristic of patristic rather than mediaeval theology. That Valla subscribed to these ideas, not merely out of political expedience in deference to his antipapal patron King Alfonso but rather in all sincerity, is demonstrated by the fact that they are found even in his ambiguously entitled oration *In Praise of St. Thomas Aquinas* (1457) written at the end of his life when he had successfully attained independence and security.

Analysis of *The Profession of the Religious*

In the dialogue entitled *The Profession of the Religious* the character Laurentius, who is undoubtedly Valla's spokesman, calls into question the view according to which members of religious orders were afforded special status as the exclusively "religious" and arrogated to themselves such distinctive privileges as greater rewards from God for having led a life of virtue. The unnamed Friar who expresses this attitude in the debate may represent specific contemporary theorists. The preacher Saint Bernardino of Siena (d. 1444), for one, claimed that members of religious orders lived in a purer manner than persons who chose the secular life.[15] But more probably, rather than having a specific individual in mind, as others too have hypoth-

---

[15] See Trinkaus, "Humanists on the Status of the Professional Religious," in his study (cited in the Select Bibliography), 2:651–82 (esp. 674).

esized,[16] Valla is responding to the general doctrine as codified, for instance, by the thirteenth-century Catholic theologian, Saint Thomas Aquinas, who, faced with the task of defending the new Mendicant Orders, that of the Dominicans in particular, argued that doing good in fulfillment of a religious vow made the action more meritorious. To Valla, instead, it seemed that the piety of the laity, if founded on inner religious fervour and on active works of charity, according to Gospel teaching, is at least equal to, and perhaps even more laudable than, religion practised sometimes perfunctorily or under constraint by friars and monks who slavishly followed the Rule of their Order.

The key phrase spoken in the treatise is perhaps the following: "It is not the external man but the inner one who pleases God" (X)—a statement that must not be misinterpreted. Although it emphasizes the role of the inner man and downplays external cult, it has little to do with the Protestant tenets of justification by faith and universal priesthood. In spite of his strong criticism of existing religious practice, Valla continues to stress good works as a means to salvation and he accepts the Church of Rome along with its hierarchical structure and its institutions. His only wish is that these might be corrected. Valla's is not the usual type of anti-clerical literature commonly produced in the Quattrocento, by Poggio Bracciolini, for example, who, in one of his dialogues (1447–48), called friars hypocritical, lazy, and greedy. Valla offers more than a superficial and negative attack. Realizing that corruption has set in, he recommends that friars return to the evangelical standards set by their founders. He shows admiration not only for saints, including Francis of Assisi, but also for the Christian martyrs, like his namesake Saint Lawrence (Laurentius), who died for the sake of Christian truth. Even in *The Donation* with its severe chastisement of modern-day popes Valla does not reject the Church or the pope's authority. He simply exhorts the pontiff to return to the more spiritual ways of his early predecessors and of the origins of Christianity.

---

[16] After studying all the literature of the period on the subject, Fois concludes (273) that Valla is probably not attacking any one specific work; Cortesi (xl-xli) too admits that the friar probably does not represent a specific individual.

To prove his main point in *The Profession* the author has recourse to the authoritative words of the Bible where he finds a definition that suits his purpose: in James 1:26–27, religion is said to consist of active charity and inner purity. Valla relies most heavily, though, not on authority, albeit a divine one, but on the semantic and etymological analysis of key terms. He finds that it was only in the Middle Ages (cf. Aquinas's usage) that the noun *religious* had been restricted to denote members of a religious community. Since in Classical Latin it had designated "pious" or "God-fearing" persons in general, Valla insists on recovering the original meaning of the word, concerned as he says he is, not merely "with the question of elegance of expression, but also with its propriety" (IV).

A major portion of the treatise is devoted to disputing the value traditionally attributed to religious vows. According to Thomistic doctrine, the professing of vows was deemed to be a religious act in itself that increased one's devotion to God. Drastically simplifying Aquinas's belaboured analysis of the modalities of vows from twelve points of inquiry (ranging from the first, "What is a vow?," to the last, "Whether the authority of a superior is required in a dispensation from a vow?"), Valla begins with a philological discussion of the polyvalent term *vow* as noun and verb, in Latin and Greek. Citing carefully selected passages from Virgil and the Bible where the word *votum* appears, he demonstrates that vows are in reality conditional promises made to God, whereas the practice of those entering religious orders involves superfluous oaths (often condemned in the Bible) that are added to promises even though the pledges should be binding in themselves. As proof that vows and oaths ought not to be equated, Valla presents arguments that skilfully exploit the syntactical features of certain verses from the Vulgate.

When the Friar, on the other hand, desperately attempts to salvage his position in the debate by distinguishing between conditional and unconditional vows, he is accused of indulging in fatuous scholastic hair-splitting that is disallowed in the discussion. What Laurentius proposes, in substitution for erroneous conceptions and defective reasoning, is a more profound meaning of *vovere* ("to vow"), one associated with the verb *devovere* ("to dedicate"), signifying a special dedication of oneself to God. Although Saint Thomas too had used this etymology, the mediaeval philosopher attached importance to external rites and the solemnizing of one's promises—acts that appear irrelevant to Valla.

Proceeding to dispute the validity of each of the three specific vows in turn, Valla has his protagonist argue that obedience, according to Cicero's use of the term (in a passage from the *Paradoxes* that has nothing to do with religion, however) can mean a shameful servility. It is much more in conformity with human dignity for one to be a ruler than a subject. Poverty is not an essential virtue either, since common sense and the most eminent of thinkers teach that it is best to avoid extremes and to provide for oneself. In this discussion Valla, in a typically humanist manner, blends Christian and pagan sources for his proof. Pressing philology into service once again, he examines the Latin and Greek etymology of the word *deacon* to show that officers in the Church hierarchy are actually "servants" and "attendants" who are expected not to live in penury but, on the contrary, to distribute aid and money to the needy. As for the third promise—chastity—it can be practised even by lay persons, whereas the vow of celibacy made by members of religious orders does not, in fact, guarantee purity at all. The general conclusion, then, is that vows are of no special merit; they are redundant because, right from Baptism, Christians are committed to lead a holy life and to obey God's commandments.

There may be flaws both in Valla's philological argumentation, because it is highly reductive, and in his use of quotations, because it is conveniently selective. Yet the basic motivation indicates an important humanist approach to religion in as much as the discussion, while including criticism of the faults of the so-called religious, also aims at exalting the devotion of lay persons and establishing secular piety on firm grounds.

The effectiveness of Valla's message lies not only in his pleas for reform themselves but also in the particular way in which he formulates his call for improvement in the organization of religious life. At the beginning of the treatise he insists that it is not purely the subject matter dealt with in a text that determines its worth, but equally the manner in which the author treats his topic. Using a number of vivid analogies to contrast good and bad styles of writing, he says that, even if they treat of such lowly subjects as Virgil's sheep, dogs, and bees, excellent works soar on high like eagles, and swim in the deep sea like whales. Continuing with spatial imagery suggestive of verticality and dynamism, he points out that weak compositions instead can be compared to birds that fly about the bushes or to fish that swim near the shore. Thus the mode he recommends, especially for literature dealing with ethics and religion, is that of classical oratory, already used as a model by the early Church Fathers.

Evidence for Valla's having designed his own treatise in accordance with the principles of oratory can be found in the headings which mark off certain sections of the arrangement (*dispositio*) of *The Profession*.[17] Although only the narration (*narratio*) and refutation (*refutatio*) are thus labelled, the peroration is mentioned in the body of the text, and the other parts are clearly distinguishable too, all displaying the features prescribed by Quintilian, especially in Book IV of his *Institutes of Oratory*. The introductory section of *The Profession*, including the exordium and narration, opens with an address to the judge to whom the work will eventually be sent (cf. *Inst.* IV.i.63); it attempts a modest concealment of the author's eloquence (IV.i.9), when Valla says he does not mean to place himself in the category of skillful writers; and it provides the basic information on the characters and the setting (IV.ii.2), as well as a summary of the main justification for the claims made by members of religious institutions (IV.ii.49). Moreover, the first-person narrator utters a personal denunciation of the treacherous and impious friars—a brief exclamatory phrase permitted in Quintilian's scheme (III.viii.10; IV.ii.120).

Intent on moving his reader as well as instructing and entertaining him, according to the dictates of classical rhetoric, Valla, in the central part of the debate that constitutes the proof (*confirmatio*), marshals his arguments, he says, as one would draw up a line of battle. For this verbal duel he adopts, quite appropriately, the dialogue genre dear to Plato, Cicero, and Augustine. It was often imitated by Renaissance humanists who, by virtue of their anti-dogmatic philosophy, preferred to air differing views on a single question (and perhaps avoid direct identification with any one position).[18] Valla creates the illusion of objectivity by eliminating direct intervention of the narrative voice in the body of the dialogue so that, as he states, perhaps following the example of Plato, Cicero, and Petrarch, "those who read it may think not that they are reading

---

[17] Cortesi (lxxii-lxxvi) has analyzed the rhetorical form of *De professione*.

[18] See David Marsh (cited in the Select Bibliography) on the dialogue in the fifteenth century.

an author, but that they are watching and listening to two disputants" (II).

Throughout the treatise Valla artfully manipulates the discussion
which, held in the public hall adjacent to the square, is essentially
a court battle. The Friar is described as a particularly learned individual who has studied both philosophy and theology extensively.
Being the more erudite of the two interlocutors, it might have been
expected that he would represent the Socratic master in the dialogue. Ironically it is Laurentius, a relative amateur, who plays the
leading role. He acquires even greater stature as a hero by means of
his name which, in addition to being that of the author, recalls the
deacon Saint Lawrence—referred to on several occasions (X, XII)—
one of the early martyrs who was active in the charitable distribution
of Church funds and achieved sainthood for his defence of high
principles. Laurentius dominates the discussion, mustering to his
cause a wide array of tactics: he asks leading questions to disprove
the Friar's arguments and to induce his opponent to make conces-
sions in a few areas concerning meritorious actions; he also changes
the subject or postpones the examination of certain issues when it
suits him—for the sake of logic, he cleverly claims. On the other
hand, the Friar's is a poor performance. Made to present weak and
exaggerated statements,[19] he becomes confused and admits he is
baffled. Generally appearing foolish as he argues in circles, he
stubbornly repeats the same point, namely, that since a more severe
punishment awaits the religious if they sin, they will receive a more
generous reward if they refrain from sin—an argument from contraries (cf. Quintilian V.x.1–2) that Laurentius refutes effectively
with an overwhelming variety of proofs. The Friar's limited ability
ultimately serves the purposes of Laurentius, whose point of view
can thus more easily prevail. As a result the paradoxical roles
assigned to the speakers suggest that philosophy and theology are
futile without the support of the inventive, structural, and stylistic
force of rhetoric. Whereas the Friar has recourse to doctrines that
have the stamp of authority for particular groups only, Laurentius

---

[19] Fois (277) has pointed out how the Friar fails to use those arguments that
would have been available to him to defend his point of view; for example, a
Biblical passage (Acts 18:18) would have supported the idea of the validity of
vows.

draws more artfully upon analogies from everyday experience that have a greater universality and appear to conform more closely to Quintilian's precept of proving the uncertain by reference to the certain (I.vi.4). It is useless, Laurentius proposes, to take vows, or to add oaths to promises already made to God, since one cannot "make healthier that which is healthy…or more perfect that which is perfect" (VII). To destroy the Friar's basic argument by contraries on the question of punishment and reward, Laurentius effectively presents (and repeats for his supposedly forgetful opponent) the analogy of doctors, who receive great praise for curing difficult diseases, but little praise in easy cases. Consequently, the religious, even though they are punished severely if they sin, do not receive any special consideration from God for keeping their promise to live virtuously.

Medical imagery such as this abounds in Valla's text, at times as a subtle expression of criticism against friars. It is implied that the medicine provided by vows may be needed, but only if the brothers have some latent illness or weakness that needs to be corrected. Other instances of offensive innuendo emerge from the figurative language adopted by Laurentius who, quoting Terence, accuses the obdurate Friar of being "stuck in the same old mud" (VI) and uses the uncomplimentary simile of a snake to describe the triadic division (*partitio*) of the Friar's argument (V). At times the satire is more direct: Laurentius notes, for example, using a typical antithetical parallelism, that many who enter convents as thin doves subsequently turn into fat pigeons. Not only these allusions to creatures from the natural world, but even a comparison with philosophers is transformed into insult, as Laurentius likens the numerous religious orders to the sects that abound in the field of philosophy. Coming from someone like Valla who finds philosophers insufferable because they reserve for themselves exclusively the appellation of "wise men," when in fact legislators, rulers, and orators too are wise (IV), this is no attempt at flattery. In addition, by means of impersonation (dealt with by Quintilian, III.viii.51–54), the protagonist twice assumes the authoritative *persona* of an ancient theologian (VII), resurrected for the purpose of directing some words of admonishment against the erring Friar. The fictitious theologian himself delivers a more passionate tirade, brief as it is, than the ineffectual pronouncements of the official spokesman for religion. In this dialogue within a dialogue, it is again ironically the layman who, as he lends his voice to the ancient theologian, proves to be more conversant with patristic traditions.

Historical examples too, recommended by Quintilian (III.viii.66), allow the protagonist to wax eloquent at the Friar's expense and much to his chagrin. Laurentius cites the expedient devised by Demosthenes, who overcame an unbecoming nervous twitch by hanging a lance dangerously over his shoulder, and he compares it to Marius's intrinsic self-restraint—a principal virtue in Valla's scheme—when he underwent leg surgery without allowing himself to be tied down. These actions, recorded by the classics, are intended to represent two ways of achieving religious goals: through fear, as do members of orders, or out of willpower, as do laymen.

One deceptively simple *exemplum* involves Anaximenes of Lampsacus. Laurentius narrates how Alexander the Great, as he was about to attack the city of Lampsacus, was filled with consternation to see Anaximenes appear. Fearing his former master would dissuade him from carrying out the assault, he immediately burst forth with the declaration that he would *not* do what his master was about to ask of him. However, Anaximenes outwits the great conqueror with the brief statement: "I am asking you to destroy Lampsacus" (XII). This historical anecdote, which occupies a significant place at the centre of the text, encapsulates the basic structure of Valla's treatise, signalling as it does not only the power of rhetoric, but the discrepancy between superficial and superliteral meaning, the sort of gap, as the theorists explain, which is inherent not only in individual figures of rhetoric, but indeed also in the underlying shape of rhetorical compositions.[20]

Considerable ambiguity stems from the dialogue structure of the treatise itself, as well as from other features of the work. The case being presented in the trial takes the form, on the surface, of an

---

[20] See Paul De Man, "Semiology and Rhetoric," in *Allegories of Reading* (London: Yale UP, 1979), esp. 9–10 on the discrepancy between the mutually exclusive literal and figurative meanings in rhetorical texts. Paul Ricoeur, *The Rule of Metaphor: Multidisciplinary Studies on the Creation of Meaning in Language* (Toronto and Buffalo: Univ. of Toronto Press, 1977), deals with the neo-rhetorical concept of deviation, based originally on Aristotle's definition of figures of speech as instances of deviation from the ordinary usage of words (*Poetics*, 1458a-b).

oratorical defence occasioned by the exaggerated claims of members of religious orders. Indeed, in his declamatory summing up, the self-fashioned victim Laurentius stresses that his purpose has been "to act as the defender, not the accuser" (XII). Yet because it is he and his companion who utter the very first gibes against the conspiratorial friars allegedly involved in the plot and thus initially spark the debate, the work becomes an act of aggression presented in the guise of self-defence. Laurentius is determined to emerge the victor, despite his protestations of friendship and goodwill. The military images (perhaps from Quintilian) which recur in his speeches reveal his veiled intentions: e.g. "I want to refute, wound, and lay you low with another type of weapon"; "Who ever asks the enemy the reasons why he has drawn up his line of battle in a certain way?" (VI).

Suddenly toward the end of the debate, though, Laurentius, echoing Quintilian's phrase (X.i.29), describes himself as a soldier who "stands 'in line of battle'" (X) not for the cause of the secular world, but for religion, for the Church, for good friars and monks—a sort of Pauline soldier of Christ. In this modified role he declaims a lengthy peroration consisting of a hymn to friars—a long, passionate piece which none of the other characters dares to interrupt, astonished as they probably all are at this unexpected reversal. Laurentius's laudatory comments include the following: "Friars are those who truly support the tottering temple of God,…those who…turn men and women away from sin, freeing them from false beliefs and leading them to piety and knowledge" (XII).

Through these epideictic elements of praise, which counterbalance the criticisms heaped on the friars heretofore, Valla may wish to show that he is equipped to argue on both sides of the question (cf. Quintilian V.xiii.44). They are similar, furthermore, to the ambivalent oration Valla later delivered supposedly as an encomium to Saint Thomas Aquinas, but which in essence censured the saint indirectly by bestowing lavish praise on the Fathers of the Church instead. However, the fundamental structure of the debate being that of judicial not demonstrative oratory, some critical assessment and a definitive decision are required. The bystanders who are present during the discussion remain doubtful, since Laurentius, their favourite throughout, ends his discourse with the unexpected paean. The bilateral debate between Laurentius and the Friar is not resolved from within either. Their conflicting viewpoints are never reconciled, not even in the form of an eclectic compromise, such as the one which brings *The True Good* to an end. Both speakers retain their convictions rigidly. The unyielding Friar refuses to concede his defeat: although he can not be master, he refuses the role of disciple or initiate. At this point, therefore, Laurentius chooses to bring the discussion to a halt with the words "faciamus pares," an Italianate phrase meaning "let us call it a draw" (XII). And because the Friar, who has requested time out for reflection, leaves and then fails to turn up on a second specified day to continue the discussion, the question remains open.

This unsettled dispute should allow the spectator-reader to judge for himself. Nevertheless, the author-narrator reveals that the audience he envisages does not include readers alone. Addressing a split receptor, he announces that a transcript of the proceedings is to be "brought for examination to the person designated" (XIII). Suddenly the dialogue which has been presented as a fluid conversation turns into a definitive text, which is to be sent to a judge. The identity of this absentee judge has suggestive connotations too: Baptista Platamon, a highly respected magistrate in King Alfonso's court, is a secular figure, called upon here to pass judgment on what is essentially a religious topic. Certainly this choice, desired and approved by all the characters in *The Profession*, is meant to direct the audience's sympathy towards the lay protagonist Laurentius. Thus the open ending is only an illusion: the judge has yet to be consulted, but his opinion can already be foreseen.

A further and rather unusual type of discrepancy and ambivalence relates to the title of the work. The official one, prefixed to the text, is neutral, and it contrasts sharply with the discarded one suggested to Laurentius as he turns scribe. When one of the participants denounces the laudatory tribute Laurentius has paid to friars because it results in logical incoherence and reveals moral weakness on the part of the discussant, he dares Laurentius, who, he says, should have brought his speech to a climax with a forceful denunciation of friars, to transcribe the disputation exactly as it took place and to entitle the text "On the False Name and Privilege of the Religious." Laurentius dismisses his critic's challenge and rejects what he calls that "terrible title although it is perhaps an accurate one" (XII), adopting instead the innocuous one that has come down to us. However, as Valla, by means of the figure of ironical negation (*paraleipsis, praeteritio,* or *antiphrasis,* as Quintilian terms it,

IX.ii.47–48), paradoxically includes in the text what he says he has decided to exclude, the memory of the original contentious title is made to linger in our minds.

Analysis of *The Donation of Constantine*

Certainly the most striking of all Valla's compositions is the treatise demonstrating the falsity of the legend of the donation of Constantine. It was an age-old belief that the Emperor Constantine the Great (d. 337) had donated temporal power to Sylvester I, Bishop of Rome (314–35), after recovering from leprosy. This gift, supposedly granted back in the fourth century, was the justification many popes of the late Middle Ages had cited, either sincerely or through guile, for their intervention in political affairs and their claim to the right to investiture. However, the document reporting the alleged donation or privilege, that is the *Constitutum Constantini* charter, was actually drawn up in the eighth century, probably in Rome, and an abridged version of it was incorporated into Church law, through Palea's interpolations, four hundred years later in the mid-twelfth century. The document consisted of a series of declarations which Constantine supposedly made in the year 313; in them he stated the primacy of the Church of Rome and of its head, declared the power of the pope to be superior to that of the emperor, announced his decision to transfer the seat of the empire to Byzantium, and granted land and other privileges to Sylvester. Although scholars before Valla had, like Dante, questioned the legality of the donation and denounced its disastrous effects on the spiritual role of the Church,[21] it was Valla who provided definitive and exhaustive proof that the document was indeed spurious and that the donation had never taken place. Some brief evidence of its apocryphal nature had been presented earlier by Nicholas of Cusa, for one, but he had buried it within an accommodating work of his (*On Catholic Harmony* of 1433) which advocated the reconciliation between emperor and

---

[21] For discussions in the Middle Ages on the validity of the Donation of Constantine and the problem of the relation between the Papacy and the Empire, see Ewart Lewis, *Medieval Political Ideas* (London: Routledge and Kegan Paul, 1954), 2:444–47 and passim.

pope. As a result his view had little impact on the resolution of the problem.

Valla, on the other hand, gathers together some old arguments and many new ones, and provides a thorough discussion of the issue. In the partition which follows the exordium of his treatise (II, 6), he outlines the seven main points he will treat: the absurdity and implausibility of the transaction, the lack of historical evidence, the similarity with other events, the location of the text in the interpolations rather than in the body of Gratian's *Decretum* (the collection of Church laws or *Harmony of the Canon*), the presence of anachronisms, and the impossibility of reclaiming title on the basis of either civil or canon law. Even though there are some limitations to his work (Valla does not deal with the identity of the author or the geographical origin of the forgery—questions which modern scholars have debated), he does present all his data in a tract which is structured in such a way as to exploit to the maximum the perlocutionary potential of the text. He admits at the very beginning of his treatise that he is being altogether revolutionary in attacking current beliefs upheld by papal authority. Nevertheless, claiming the right to dissent, he speaks out courageously and explains: "My purpose is not to inveigh against any person....Rather, I seek to eradicate error from men's minds" (I, 4). In his usual search for the truth, he states that he has carried out a careful examination of ancient sources and of various mediaeval manuscripts of the *Decretum*, only to discover that contemporary accounts of the period had recorded no donation and that the oldest compilations of Church law did not contain the charter in question.

In addition to the conclusions reached, what is of utmost significance in this work of Valla's, as in *The Profession of the Religious*, is the method—philological and at the same time rhetorical—by means of which he argues his case. He devotes almost one-third of the treatise (32 of a total of 99 paragraphs, from XII, 38 to XXII, 69) to a careful analysis of the text of the donation document almost word by word. As he proceeds, he detects a number of cultural anachronisms, linguistic discrepancies, and geographical oddities in it. Among the references made to the customs and attire of the protagonists involved in the alleged granting of power, the charter refers to the pope's bejewelled diadem when, in fact, silk caps were still worn by pontiffs at the time. The word *datum* (given or dated) appears in a closing phrase of the text, when such usage was reserved for the drafting of letters to be delivered to a specific addressee. The mention of Constantinople too is an obvious blunder, he finds, since the city had not yet been founded and at that time the site was known as Byzantium. Along with examples of grammatical barbarisms, Valla detects implausible linguistic practice in words like *satraps*, alien to the vocabulary employed in the fourth century to describe the political organization of the Empire. He uses similar philological evidence to support other arguments too: through the analysis of the history, etymology, and usage of key terms, he is able to demonstrate, for example, that since the designation *clergy* in its Greek etymology means "lot" or "portion," in the sense of "destiny," Sylvester, whose lot as bishop of Rome was a supremely celestial one, could not have accepted Constantine's gift. So even the use of this expression, let alone the idea of the transaction itself, undermines the forger's credibility.

As for the general structure of the charter's narrative content, Valla deduces that the tale of the donation smacks of a rewriting of the biblical story of Naaman the Syrian who, cured by Elisha, offered him gifts. This similarity, along with the fact that the story of Constantine's conversion recalls parts of the early legend of Sylvester,[22] points to the inherently mythical quality of the charter.

Besides the internal evidence provided by the language and form of the charter text, Valla discovers that there is a lack of external documentation which could support the view that the donation had taken place for, not only did historical works written at the time of the donation make no mention of the event, but neither had any coins commemorating it come down. Valla offers other arguments relating to external matters: from a legal standpoint, it would have been contrary to human law for the emperor to have carried out such a transfer of power, and also contrary to divine law for the pope to have accepted. Moreover, even if it had occurred, the papacy could no longer expect to reclaim its lost power by law. From the

---

[22] Sylvester was believed to have assisted Constantine in his conversion after the emperor rejected the advice of pagan priests urging him to bathe in the blood of infants in order to rid himself of leprosy. The details of this and other legends are discussed in Christopher Bush Coleman, *Constantine the Great and Christianity. Three Phases: The Historical, the Legendary and the Spurious* (New York: n.p., 1914), 161–64.

point of view of verisimilitude, then, the notion of a donation is highly unlikely. Valla's analysis, based on the rhetorical criterion of common-sense plausibility and on that of human experience and behaviour, as has been observed,[23] takes psychological factors into account too. It is part of human nature to be acquisitive, and rulers invariably aim at enlarging their territory, not at giving it away. "But why do you declare as being credible that which is contrary to the opinion of men?" Valla asks at one point in his discussion (VIII, 28).

The cogency of Valla's arguments is evident. But, as is the case with *The Profession*, written in dialogue form, what makes this treatise on the donation highly convincing is the presence of verbal strategies, true speech acts, with which the author elects to do battle against the credulous. Utilizing classical rhetorical devices, like dramatized speeches, that had become essential writing instruments for the humanists, he structures his work as an "oration," as he calls it (III, 7 and XXX, 99), one to be inscribed more precisely under the rubric of judicial oratory, as one critic has pointed out.[24] As to its specific nature, Valla states in a letter that his work on the donation is one long dispute.[25] It is not surprising, therefore, that the sixteenth-century publishers of the text should have entitled it a "declamation."

Indeed, rather than a straightforward third-person discussion Valla's work takes the shape of an inquiry during the course of which the prosecutor-narrator calls a group of witnesses, dead and alive, to testify in the case (or *causa*, as he terms it [XXII, 70]). As a rhetorically structured transcript of the court proceedings addressed to the kings and princes of his time, the treatise reports a series of fictitious speeches delivered, in the first two instances, by the sorrowful members of the emperor's family, who plead with the emperor not to deprive them of their inheritance, and by representatives of the government of Rome who come forward to voice their anger over the loss of territory and power. These impersonations serve to explain, in human terms, the feelings and motives of the various actors who would have been involved in this living drama.

---

[23] De Caprio (see Select Bibliography) provides an excellent study of the norms of behaviour which constitute the fundamental criterion on which Valla bases his arguments.

[24] De Caprio, 45

[25] Letter to Guarino Veronese (1443), in *Epistole*, 245.

The interrogation focusses generally on the imagined testimony of those who uphold the truthfulness of the donation and of the forger himself who, it is said, should be "drag[ged] into court" (XI, 37). Displaying a great deal of moral indignation the investigator subjects them to rigid questioning with such vehemence that the interrogatives he formulates are not the usual, sometimes bland kind of rhetorical questions; they take on, instead, the force of real verbal abuse. The prosecutor stresses how wrong and improbable it would have been for the donation to have taken place, and, furthermore, how utterly absurd it was for anyone to believe it had. In a particularly vituperative tone, he accuses the forger of being dishonest, an evil villain, and a stupid ass, and his credulous contemporaries, of being mad, ridiculous, ignorant fools. He hurls these insults like lethal weapons in his attempt, as he explains, "to deal the fatal blow to [his] adversaries' cause, which has already been beaten and torn to bits, and to slit its throat with a single slash" (X, 34). Valla characteristically uses a remarkable number of such military images throughout the treatise,[26] in the tradition of Quintilian and Saint Paul. Making words his verbal weapons, he attacks the gullible with irony too, as in the punning passage: "Oh, what an astonishing event! The Roman Empire…was both acquired and lost by Christian priests so calmly and quietly….You would think that *Sylvester* had reigned in *sylvan* places amid trees, rather than in Rome among men" [emphasis added] (VIII, 30).

Interestingly enough, all these forms of verbal aggression are used in a context which is presented as an act of self-defence. At the outset the narrator-lawyer depicts himself as a victim who finds himself in a situation similar to that of the biblical heroes Jeremiah and Saint Paul, forced to defend the truth against evil aggressors. Using a sort of rhetoric of deviation reminiscent of that found in *The Profession*, he veils with a defensive surface cover what is in effect a violent attack of his own. Other instances of this strategy include the figure of preterition used to attenuate the denunciation of priests and the high praise of the holy pope towards the end which recalls, by contrast, his sharp criticism of contemporary counterparts (XXVIII, 93–XXIX, 94). Valla first denounces the tyranny of priests who, at one time good shepherds, had subsequently exploited the

---

[26] This imagery has been analyzed by Fois, 481.

superstitions of the people and had become "thieves and bandits" (XXVI, 85). Comparing recent popes to the tyrannical Caesars who usurped republican freedom, he decries the loss of liberty as well as the improper use of Church funds to wage war rather than to help the poor and, on the other hand, highlights the spirituality of the holy popes of the past. Glowing praise is reserved for Sylvester, in particular, who is called "a most holy man" (XXX, 98; cf. "holy man," VII, 27). In the drama performed before us, Valla gives him an eminently noble role to play and lines to recite that are filled with devotion. References that the author makes to papal "dignity" and "majesty" at the beginning and in the closing phrase of the work (II, 5; XXX, 99) serve to frame the topic of true evangelical and orthodox religiosity, which is at the very heart of the debate that is enacted.

Valla has his protagonist-narrator-champion clinch one round of the courtroom battle with a passionate apostrophe to none other than Christ who, he prays, will "hurl avenging thunderbolts" against the perpetrator of the horrendous falsification (XV, 49). By fashioning his work as a series of such addresses to specific individuals (popes, kings, Constantine, the credulous, the forger and so on) Valla creates a sense of immediate orality and direct communication. Dramatic scenes are recited too, as when Sylvester speaks directly to Constantine and turns down his diabolical gift, quoting the words of Christ and Paul from the Bible in support of his refusal (VI, 20–21). In another instance, the lawyer asks the person responsible for the charter proclamations, if he is indeed Constantine, to give the reasons for his strange statements (XIX, 62). The stress on speech is evident, furthermore, in the fact that the entire treatise is one long oration, organized into clearly discernible parts extending from exordium to peroration, according to the traditional scheme, and ending with a final exhortation that the pope will once again be the vicar of Christ alone and not also of Caesar. Valla's rhetorical text includes other, briefer discourses—those of the characters already mentioned, whose speeches, in turn, often contain quotations from other texts. Even the imaginary objectors incessantly repeat the phrase, "The Church of Rome gained possession through prescription" (XXVIII, 89–90). Their stubborn insistence enlivens the often technical legal discussion that Valla includes in his treatment of the matter. And, of course, the spoken declarations of the charter are cited phrase by phrase by the prosecutor in his interrogation of the forger. What emerges from this speech-within-a-speech-within-a-speech formation is a multilayered dialogue, which not only presents a multitude of argumentative approaches, but also highlights textuality and discourse in its very design.

Each segment, moreover, is directed to one specifically named person or group of persons, addressed as "you," yet the second-person pronoun, even as it is continually displaced from character to character, inevitably impacts on the implied audience outside the text. The reader, though addressed indirectly, is thus engaged in the debate. Furthermore, as the discourse alternates between the second and third persons, when the prosecutor refers to the forger as "you" and then shifts suddenly and often with insulting tones to "he" (e.g. XII, 38), clearly directing his remarks to the general audience, it is evident that the audience is being called upon to pass judgment in the trial. What the result will be is no mystery: the receiver of the text cannot help but share the scorn heaped by the narrator on the foolish forger and also wish to establish distance from the ingenuous believers repeatedly and sarcastically held up to ridicule for their stupidity.

On the basis of these features *The Donation*, like *The Profession*, clearly achieves the goal of effective persuasion. The sheer number of arguments, and the forcefulness of each, together with the high emotional charge created by the various discursive strategies, make the total effect quite overwhelming. In addition to providing an unabashed expression of the author's religious views, a skilful solution to a textual puzzle, and the debunking of the most famous forgery in history, the treatise also shows in a concrete way the power that the text has to attack and interrogate, insult and humiliate, indeed to overcome and conquer. And although it may carry out these actions only through perlocution, in a verbal, quasi-fictional manner, and in order to defeat an earlier text, it ultimately achieves its humanist goal of affecting man's perception of truth and altering his way of thinking.

Valla himself had stated (*On Pleasure*, 87) that rhetoric is to be employed, not simply to win debates, but in order to reach the truth. The orator must be a moral individual, as the rhetoricians of antiquity had taught, so that rhetoric would not be made to serve dishonest ends. Certainly he practised what he preached in this sense, using his knowledge of language and of oratorical techniques in order to clarify concepts and to tackle in a committed and honest way what were the more worrisome questions of the day. A superb philologist, he passes knowledgeably from the word (*verbum*) to the thing it signifies (*res*), making major contributions to Renaissance thought and scholarship.

Evidence of the complexity of Valla's works and of the richness of his ideas can be found in the variety of interpretations accorded him and his writings in critical assessments produced over the centuries from his age to our own. The early Protestants eagerly claimed him as their precursor whereas in Italy, during his lifetime, he was denounced as a heretic by certain Church officials and some of his works were eventually placed on the Index of Prohibited Books. During the period of the unification of Italy he was seen both as a proponent of anticlericalism (a view that has been revived in a recent reprint of Pepe's Italian translation claiming relevance to the ongoing struggle between Church and State) and as a prophet of the Church's submission to the modern Italian state, while twentieth-century Catholic critics (Di Napoli and Fois) stress the religious orthodoxy of his views. From the point of view of his contribution to the field of learning, scholars of the Renaissance (Erasmus) and of recent times (Garin, Gaeta, Vasoli, Gray, Camporeale) have considered him to be the true founder of humanist philology and the reformer of rhetoric. In the area of the history of ideas, Kristeller and Trinkaus have illustrated the important place Valla occupies in Renaissance philosophy and theology and attribute to him the re-establishment of rhetorical theology based on persuasion rather than demonstration. Finally, readers of a linguistic bent (Gerl, Waswo, Streuver) have concentrated on his philosophy of language and have compared his views on the influential role of language in shaping human thought to those of the philosophers Vico and Wittgenstein.

Critics have also taken different approaches in their analyses of the two treatises included here. Many, as indicated above, have appreciated the philological methods adopted by Valla. Some, including Radetti, have emphasized his contribution to the religious thought of the Renaissance; *The Profession* is interpreted by Fois, for example, as an illustration of the various ways to reach God. On the other hand, some readers have doubted the sincerity of the views expressed and have reduced the tracts to forms of pro-Aragonese propaganda (see Fois on *The Donation*) and Valla to little more than a subservient courtier (see Guidi on *The Profession*).

The present revised edition is intended to provide the texts of the two treatises in English (the first in its entirety and the second through selections) and to furnish the background information needed to place them in their historical context. It aims, moreover, to illustrate how, as a rhetorician in the classical tradition, Valla successfully elaborated verbal constructs that serve not only as examples of the discrepancy and deviation factors that constitute the inner mechanisms of the rhetorical medium, but also as illustrations of texts that made a direct impact on the reality of the day through the persuasive power of the word. Even if time and change have necessarily tempered our emotional response to the specific issues that Valla raises, we continue to derive pleasure and profit as we engage in an intellectual dialogue with one of the more acute minds of fifteenth-century Italy.

Translator's Note

This complete English translation of *De professione religiosorum* was originally based on the edition by J. Vahlen published in 1869 and photostatically reproduced in Valla's *Opera omnia*, edited by Garin in 1962. The following were also consulted: a partial Italian version together with the corresponding Latin text by E. Garin, G. Radetti's complete Italian translation, and a few passages rendered into English by C. Trinkaus in his study on humanist thought. A number of the emendations to the Latin text suggested by Vahlen and Garin were incorporated, the major ones being *misereantur* "feeling pity" instead of *irascantur* "getting angry" (I), and *Jonas* "Jonah" instead of *Ioannes* "John" (VIII).

In the present edition a few minor textual changes have been made to the translation in light of the revised readings given in M. Cortesi's critical edition, which appeared in 1986 and which was based on the sole extant manuscript of the work in the Vatican Library (Urb. Lat., MS. 595, fols. 1–25r). Further modifications in the translation stem from suggestions made by various readers and reviewers of the first and second editions. In its formal presentation, the text has been divided into brief chapters according to the scheme adopted by Cortesi, but without her further subdivision of it into paragraphs. It should be noted that the headings, designed to highlight the topic under discussion or the oratorical division of the treatise, though they may appear somewhat incomplete and inconsistent, are those found in the manuscript and/or in Cortesi's edition. In accordance with the Vatican codex (originally consulted directly for the first edition), the narration and the refutation are indicated in the titles, whereas the exordium, the proof, and the peroration are not.

The translation seeks to be as faithful as possible to the original and to retain the vivid imagery typical of Valla's style, without, however, sacrificing a concern for the features of acceptable English prose. Minor flaws in the two principal existing versions of *De professione* in Italian were eliminated and new interpretations provided for *de eiusdem difficillima quaque materia*, rendered here as "even in the most difficult of its subject areas" (I), *agapetae* "spiritual brethren" (IV) (see note to the text), *a contrario* "by means of an argument from contraries" (V), and *faciamus pares* "let us call it a draw" (XII).

De falso credita et ementita Constantini donatione, unlike *De professione*, has been printed many times and has been the object of a great number of studies. The most recent critical edition by W. Setz which appeared in 1976 was the basis for this translation. The text included in the present revised edition has been augmented; it now amounts to approximately thirty per cent of the original text and omissions are indicated with ellipses. A complete English translation of the treatise by Coleman and Italian versions by Pepe, Radetti, and myself, the first two of which were produced before the critical edition appeared, however, may be consulted by those wishing to read the work in its entirety.

The Introduction and Select Bibliography have been revised and augmented to incorporate more recent developments in Valla criticism. My studies on the two treatises composed separately after the issuing of the first edition of this translation have been partially incorporated in the analyses provided in the Introduction. For the quotations from the classics that are frequently cited by Valla in both treatises, published translations have been drawn upon and are acknowledged in the notes. When these were not available or did not adhere closely enough to the original, or to Valla's sometimes inexact citing of it, new versions have been furnished. The King James version of *The Holy Bible* (New York: New American Library, 1974) has been used for the frequent references to the Vulgate. Wherever possible these are given in parentheses in the text. However, some modifications have been unavoidable, especially in order to render Valla's philological arguments more clearly in English. In all cases, notes or square brackets mark departures from the text quoted.

Special thanks go to the readers of this translation for their suggestions, namely, Professor Emeritus David F.S. Thomson of the Department of Classics of the University of Toronto, who checked the translation in an early draft for the first edition, Professor Erika Rummel of the Department of History of Wilfrid Laurier University, who carefully read the whole manuscript in its revised form, and especially Professor Charles Fantazzi of the Department of Classical and Modern Languages of the University of Windsor, who subjected the translations to a very rigorous examination. Invaluable advice on specific textual problems was provided by Professors Giancarlo Alessio of the University of Venice and Vito R. Giustiniani of the University of Freiburg im Br. I have benefitted from further suggestions by Professor John Monfasani of the State University of New York at Albany. Of course, the responsibility for any remaining errors is completely mine. I am particularly grateful to the members of the Centre for Reformation and Renaissance Studies (Victoria College, University of Toronto), and to the library staff at the Centre, for their assistance and to the previous President of Victoria, Professor Eva Kushner, for generously providing a grant for two former research assistants, Robert Buranello and Ian Martin, who helped in a number of ways with the preparation of the second edition.

Select Bibliography

Works by Valla

Opera omnia. Ed. Eugenio Garin. 2 vols. Turin: Bottega d'Erasmo, 1962.

De professione religiosorum. Ed. J. Vahlen, 99–134. Sitzungsberichte der Kaiserlichen Akademie der Wissenschaften (Vienna), Philosophisch-Historische Classe, 62 (1869), and photostatically reproduced in Valla, *Opera* (1962), 2:287–322.

De professione religiosorum. Ed. Mariarosa Cortesi. Padua: Antenore, 1986.

De falso credita et ementita Constantini donatione. Ed. Wolfram Setz. Monumenta Germaniae Historica, vol. 10. Weimar: Hermann Böhlaus Nachfolger, 1976.

Prosatori latini del Quattrocento. Ed. Eugenio Garin. Milan-Naples: Ricciardi, 1952. Includes *De professione eligiosorum* (*Degli ordini religiosi*), *De libero arbitrio* (*Il libero arbitrio*) and the Prefaces to *Elegantiarum libri* (*Le eleganze*).

Scritti filosofici e religiosi. Trans. Giorgio Radetti. Florence: Sansoni, 1953. Includes: *Del vero e del falso bene; Dialogo intorno al libero arbitrio; Discorso sulla falsa e menzognera Donazione di Costantino; Dialogo intorno alla professione dei religiosi; Apologia ad Eugenio IV; In lode di S. Tommaso d'Aquino.*

The Treatise on the Donation of Constantine. Trans. Christopher B. Coleman. New Haven: Yale UP, 1922. Includes the critical edition of the donation charter. Rpt. Toronto: Univ. of Toronto Press, 1993.

La falsa donazione di Costantino (contro il potere temporale dei papi). Trans. Gabriele Pepe. Milan: Universale Economica, 1952. Rpt. Florence: Ponte alle Grazie editori, 1992.

La falsa donazione di Costatino. Ed. and trans. Olga Pugliese. Milan: BUR Rizzoli, 1994.

Arte della grammatica. Ed. Paola Casciano. Milan: Fondazione Lorenzo Valla and Arnoldo Mondadori Editore, 1990.

Epistole. Ed. Ottavio Besomi and Mariangela Regoliosi. Padua: Antenore, 1984.

In Praise of St. Thomas Aquinas. In *Renaissance Philosophy: New Translations*, ed. Leonard A. Kennedy. The Hague: Mouton, 1973.

On Free Will. Trans. Charles E. Trinkaus. In *The Renaissance Philosophy of Man*, ed. E. Cassirer et al. Chicago: Univ. of Chicago Press, 1948.

On Free Will. In *Renaissance Philosophy*, vol. 1 (*The Italian Philosophers*), ed. and trans. Arturo B. Fallico and Herman Shapiro. New York: Modern Library, 1967.

On Pleasure (*De Voluptate*). Trans. A. Kent Hieatt and Maristella Lorch. New York: Abaris Books, 1977. Contains a useful introduction in English.

Works on Valla

Antonazzi, Giovanni. *Lorenzo Valla e la polemica sulla donazione di Costantino.* Rome: Edizioni di Storia e Letteratura, 1985.

Barber, Joseph A. "Lorenzo Valla e la critica attributiva: analisi della *Declamatio* umanistica contro la *Donazione di Costantino.*" *Italienisch* 16 (1986): 56–66.

Barozzi, Luciano and Remigio Sabbadini. *Studi sul Panormita e sul Valla.* Pubblicazioni del R. Istituto di Studi superiori pratici e di Perfezionamento in Firenze, Sezione di filosofia e filologia, Pubblicazioni, vol. 35. Florence: Le Monnier, 1891.

Boba, Imre. "La *Donatio Constantini* e l'*Oratio* del Valla a confronto." *Angelicum* 67 (1990): 215–39.

Camporeale, Salvatore I. *Lorenzo Valla. Umanesimo e teologia.* Florence: Istituto Nazionale di Studi sul Rinascimento, 1972.

———. "Lorenzo Valla, *Repastinatio, liber primus*: retorica e linguaggio." In *Lorenzo Valla e l'Umanesimo italiano,* ed. Ottavio Besomi and Mariangela Regoliosi, 217–39. Padua: Antenore, 1986.

———. "Per una rilettura del *De falso credita donatione* di L. Valla." In *Ambrogio Traversari nel VI centenario della nascita,* ed. Gian Carlo Garfagnini, 95–103. Florence: Leo S. Olschki Editore, 1988.

De Caprio, Vincenzo. "Retorica e ideologia nella *Declamatio* di Lorenzo Valla sulla donazione di Costantino." *Paragone* 338 (1978): 35–56.

Di Napoli, Giovanni. *Lorenzo Valla: filosofia e religione nell'Umanesimo italiano.* Rome: Edizioni di Storia e Letteratura, 1971.

Fois, Mario S.I. *Il pensiero cristiano di Lorenzo Valla nel quadro storico-culturale del suo ambiente.* Rome: Libreria Editrice dell'Università Gregoriana, 1969.

Gaeta, Franco. *Lorenzo Valla: filologia e storia nell'Umanesimo italiano.* Naples: Istituto Italiano, 1955.

Gerl, Hanna-Barbara. *Rhetorik als Philosophie: Lorenzo Valla.* Munich: Fink, 1974.

Gray, Hanna H. "Renaissance Humanism: The Pursuit of Eloquence." *Journal of the History of Ideas* 34 (1963): 497–514. Reprinted in *Renaissance Essays,* ed. P.O. Kristeller and P.P. Wiener. New York: Harper and Row, 1968. Rpt. Rochester: Univ. of Rochester Press, 1992. Deals with Valla's treatise on the donation of Constantine.

Guidi, Remo L. "Il *De professione religiosorum* di Lorenzo Valla." In *Aspetti religiosi nella letteratura del Quattrocento,* 1:79–123. Rome-Vicenza: LIEF, 1973.

Guidi, Remo L. "Lorenzo Valla e la vita dei claustrali." *Studi francescani* 87 (1990): 71–124.

Kristeller, Paul O. "Lorenzo Valla." In *Eight Philosophers of the Italian Renaissance*. Stanford, CA: Stanford UP, 1964.

Lorch, Maristella. "Lorenzo Valla." In *Renaissance Humanism*, ed. Albert Rabil Jr., 1:332–49. Philadelphia: Univ. of Pennsylvania Press, 1988.

Mancini, Girolamo. *Vita di Lorenzo Valla*. Florence: Sansoni, 1891.

Marsh, David. "Lorenzo Valla and the Rhetorical Dialogue." In *The Quattrocento Dialogue. Classical Tradition and Humanist Innovation*. Harvard Studies in Comparative Literature, vol. 35. Cambridge, MA: Harvard UP, 1980.

Monfasani, John. Review article on Cortesi's edition of *De professione* in *Rivista di letteratura italiana* 5:2 (1987): 351–65.

Monfasani, John et al. A debate on Valla's theory of language in *Journal of the History of Ideas* 50 (1989): 309–36.

Pugliese, Olga Z. "The Rhetoric of Deviation in Lorenzo Valla's *The Profession of the Religious*." *Renaissance and Reformation* n.s. 9 (1985): 263–74.

——. "The Power of the Text in Humanist Culture: Valla and the Donation of Constantine," *Scripta Mediterranea* 12–13 (1991–92): 157–68.

Seigel, Jerrold E. "Lorenzo Valla and the Subordination of Philosophy to Rhetoric." In *Rhetoric and Philosophy in Renaissance Humanism: The Union of Eloquence and Wisdom, Petrarch to Valla*. Princeton, NJ: Princeton UP, 1968.

Setz, Wolfram. *Lorenzo Vallas Schrift gegen die Konstantinische Schenkung (De falso credita et ementita Constantini donatione). Zur Interpretation und Wirkungsgeschichte*. Tübingen: Max Niemeyer, 1975.

Streuver, Nancy S. "Vico, Valla and the Logic of Humanist Inquiry." In *Giambattista Vico's Science of Humanity*, ed. Giorgio Tagliacozzo and D. P. Verene. Baltimore: Johns Hopkins UP, 1976.

Trinkaus, Charles. *"In Our Image and Likeness": Humanity and Divinity in Italian Humanist Thought*. 2 vols. London: Constable, 1970.

Vasoli, Cesare. *La dialettica e la retorica dell'Umanesimo: "invenzione" e "metodo" nella cultura del XV e XVI secolo*. Milan: Feltrinelli, 1968.

Waswo, Richard. "The 'Ordinary Language Philosophy' of Lorenzo Valla." *Bibliothèque d'Humanisme et Renaissance* 41 (1979): 255–71.

———. *Language and Meaning in the Renaissance*. Princeton, NJ: Princeton UP, 1987.

The Profession of the Religious

I

Baptista, your honour,[1] many persons often marvel at me and some even reproach me personally, partly because I tackle subjects that are too lofty and difficult, and partly because I never fail to select someone to chastise. I should gladly follow their persistent advice if they could ever really convince me. But, as for the first part of their criticisms, how is it possible for me to choose trivial themes to write about? For we do not measure a topic so much by its intrinsic nature as by the skill of the writer with the result that subjects are generally judged to be either sublime or insignificant according to the degree of the author's ability. Similarly, through the vast expanse of the air that surrounds us, we behold the birds passing to and fro, far and near, some holding a course on high close to the clouds, others a little lower, still others not far above the ground, while some restrict themselves to flying about the shrubs and bushes. The same occurs in the water also, where one species of fish likes the shores, another rocky recesses, and many enjoy the deep boundless sea. All of them inhabit one and the same element; nevertheless they differ considerably among themselves as to the variety of their habitat, since each one adapts to the place that is especially suited to it. So it is that the

---

[1] Baptista Platamon was a diplomat and counsellor in the court of King Alfonso V of Aragon and also a judge of the grand court. A man of considerable influence, he was later to become vice-chancellor to the king. See F. Marletta, "Un uomo di stato del Quattrocento: Battista Platamone," *Archivio storico per la Sicilia* 2:1 (1935): 29–68, and Cortesi, xix–xxii.

strongest among them daringly penetrate to the very heart of the element, as do the eagles in the sky, the whales in the sea.

The same law applies to the topics that man's natural inclination selects to fly and swim in, so to speak. In truth no subject is so fertile that it does not appear barren when handled by one with slim talent; none, on the contrary, is so sterile that it does not seem fruitful when treated by one endowed with rich style. For example, many have written about the Trojan war both after and, I believe, before Homer; yet Homer surpasses them all just as an eagle or a whale leaves behind all other birds or fish.[2] Virgil wrote on agriculture, vines and trees, on sheep, dogs, and bees—very lowly subjects, if one considers them in themselves, but most excellent in this author. On the contrary, when I read certain modern poets who have undertaken to sing of the wars of kings and peoples, they speak in such a way that it would have been better if, like the youthful Homer, they had sung of the battles of frogs and mice, or of those of the bees, as Virgil did. What degree of sublimity can such a subject as a shield possibly have? Yet what is more sublime than either Achilles's or Aeneas's armour as described by these authors in their poems, where it seems they are portraying, painting, and representing not a small circular shield but the orb of the earth itself? So important is the measure of ability and eloquence with which you treat your subject.

But, leaving aside poetry, let us speak of prose. Among historical writings of the same scope is there not yet such diversity due to the inequality of style of the writers, that you read, examine and reread one with an attentive, engrossed, and engaged mind, whereas you skim through the other negligently and sleepily, unable to read it through to the end? Why is this so? Because in the former it appears that great, important, and crucial matters are described; in the latter, petty, commonplace, and unimportant ones. Now, in truth, do you not see how even in the same judicial cases one orator's speech

---

[2] The works referred to are Homer's *Iliad*, Virgil's *The Georgics*, and *The Battle of the Frogs and Mice* (*Batrachomyomachia*), a mock-epic once attributed to Homer.

Achilles's shield is described in the *Iliad* as having been wrought by Hephaestus and depicting the skies, two cities, wedding festivities, wars, and country scenes (XVIII.663–843). Aeneas's shield bears sculptures by Vulcan illustrating the history of Rome (Virgil, *Aeneid*, VIII.626–731).

is passionate, while another's is cold, and when the first is speaking, the judges and the audience first become angry, then calm down; at one point they rejoice, cheer, and laugh, at another, feel pity, grieve, and weep; whereas when the other delivers his speech, they can hardly resist sleep or even succumb to it?

Leaving aside countless examples of this, I shall proceed to theology, which is the subject I am going to write about. Who, I ask, does not dare to compose works in this field, even in the most difficult of its subject areas? Thus, not without reason Horace said: "we all write poems, whether we know how to do it or not."[3] What he says of poets I apply to theologians. There is such a difference among writers of theology that, when I compare those who treat a common theme, they do not appear to be speaking on the same subject; rather, one deals with most weighty matters, another with the most insignificant; one with the stars, another with little flowers. One appears to creep, droop, sleep, snore, and dream, the other moves in felicitous flight, now, as it were, ranging the sky, then frolicking in a circle, at one time plunging in headlong descent and, at another, returning on high with the same speed.[4]

I am not saying this, of course, as though I myself possessed these laudable qualities, but simply in order to illustrate the diversity of talents that exert themselves in the same field. Clearly, those who discourse sublimely, eloquently, and with grandeur, do not necessarily owe their success to their subject matter, nor do those who express themselves aridly, feebly, and poorly derive these results from the dryness of their theme. The cause lies in the one who writes rather than in that which is written about. Therefore what the nature

---

[3] Horace, Epistle II.1 (to Augustus), v. 117, in *The Satires and Epistles of Horace*, trans. Smith Palmer Bovie (Chicago and London: Univ. of Chicago Press, 1966), 253.

[4] Quintilian had used metaphors of movement in discussing eloquence which, according to him, "must not restrict itself to narrow tracks, but range at large over open fields. Its streams must not be conveyed through narrow pipes like the water of fountains, but flow as mighty rivers flow...." *Institutio oratoria*, V.xiv.31, trans. H.E. Butler (Cambridge, MA: Harvard UP and London: William Heinemann, 1980), 2:365, 367. The classical texts cited in the note in Cortesi's edition appear to be less pertinent since the wording in them has a literal sense only.

of my topic is, and how I treat it, can be known through a comparison with the practice of others.

I shall return now to the second objection raised against me,
namely that I always choose someone to reprove. In this connection
I recently wrote a long, detailed letter of self-defence to my very
good friend Serra.[5] Nevertheless, those who expect a response from
me here should know that it has been my custom up to now, and it
will be even more so in the future, to follow the style and the
opinions of the ancient writers, both Greek and Latin, and to speak
frankly, according to their practice. Moreover, I am led to compose
this work and send it to you, Baptista, not only on my own initiative
but also on the advice of others, as you will learn from the brief tract
itself.

In it I have reported the debate I had recently with a certain friar,
whose name it seemed best not to mention, a particularly learned
individual who has studied both philosophy and theology extensively.

II

Narration

Some days ago I was standing around in a circle with several other
men of erudition in the public hall adjacent to the square. This
person, who was a close friend of all of us, approached as we
conversed and, after exchanging greetings with us, he was admitted to the group. We were discussing the conspiracy that had
been uncovered that same day, January 4th, and some disagree-
ment had arisen among us concerning this event.[6] Two days
before, a pair of wolves had been found inside the city walls and,
after a long chase through the city, they had finally been killed

---

[5] In his letter to the rhetorician Giovanni Serra [c. 1439–40] (Opera, 2:390),
Valla states that he tries to correct only those who fail to follow in the tracks of
the ancient authors, especially with respect to the proper use of Latin.
Information on Serra is available in Agostino Sottili, "Note biografiche sui
petrarchisti…e sull'umanista valenziano Giovanni Serra," in Petrarca 1304–74:
Beiträge zu Werk und Wirkung, ed. F. Schalk (Frankfurt: Klostermann, 1975),
270–86.

[6] It is not known exactly to what historical event Valla is referring.

by the people.[7] We were wondering whether this event foretold the planning of the conspiracy and its discovery. At this point Paulus Corbio[8] said: "I really do not know whether this is a portent, but who can deny that it is an ominous prodigy that some priests should have taken part in the conspiracy, and indeed a leading part, for it was before them that the conspirators swore." At this point I exclaimed: "Oh, it is a portentous and unnatural omen for anyone to have defiled consecrated hands to perform such a detestable deed, for faith to have been misused for treachery, religion for impiety, an oath for perjury, and for both divine and human affairs to have become objects of contempt and abuse." The Friar, who, as his demeanour indicated, was getting ready to reply to this, stood motionless for a while. Paulus, speaking again either to tease and provoke him or because he was truly angry, remarked: "It is a wonder that some friar was not involved in this Trojan horse, or rather, to speak more truly, that he did not devise it."[9]

The Friar in our midst, becoming more indignant, said to him: "Would you have anything to say, Paulus, if a friar was involved in and led the conspiracy? Your words indicate that you wish to arouse hostility toward the religious order itself rather than blaming the guilty friars individually, if perhaps there are some. It is as though one were to accuse all the apostles because Judas was a traitor. It has not escaped my notice how you usually think and speak ill of us. You are always the same. But if you knew how much honour, how many privileges and prerogatives there are in belonging to a religious community, you would take this

---

[7] As Cortesi has noted (p. 11n), unusual incidents regarding the sighting of wolves in the city are told by Livy in *From the Founding of the City* (e.g. III.xxix.9).

[8] This character has been identified as Pietro Paolo Corbio, a jurist in the service of King Alfonso (see Marletta, cited above in note 1, and Cortesi, xxii-xxvi). Laurentius's name also has been left in the original Latin to avoid a too literal identification of the speaker with the author that the Italian form "Lorenzo" would suggest.

[9] The wooden horse was built by the ancient Greeks during the siege of Troy as a stratagem to gain entry secretly into the city. The Greek soldiers who hid in the horse took the Trojans by surprise and caused the fall of Troy. This event is narrated in Book 2 of the *Aeneid*.

habit just as I did after I was informed of this, rather than casting abuse on it." Paulus replied: "I am not insulting your habit at all, nor am I maligning your religious order. But what, pray, are the honours, privileges, and prerogatives you refer to?" The Friar said to him: "Is it not an advantage that, although both you and I conduct our lives in a similar manner, I, nevertheless, shall receive a greater reward from God than you?" "You friars often boast of those things," said Paulus, "in order to lure others to your Order. As for me, if I had to sin, I should prefer to sin without a cowl rather than with a cowl." "And why," asked the Friar, "did you not add that it is better to do good with a cowl than without one?"[10] At this point the others laughed, yet they still remained undecided and questioned one another, and several turned to me and asked me to voice my opinion. I said, "Since we are free, do we wish to debate the issue, so that it will become clear to all which view is right?" "Do you perhaps have any doubts about it, Laurentius?" queried the Friar. "Why not," I answered, "since even Paulus does?" "I have no doubt whatsoever," quipped Paulus, "rather, I am certain that this man has wrongly boasted of the religious profession." "Still," added the Friar, "you would not have the courage to defend what you are saying." "Since you already have some one to contend with," retorted Paulus, "why do you seek another?" Then everyone in turn exhorted me and the Friar to sit down and initiate the debate.

The two of us sat down together in the middle, as they urged us to do, but on seats that were set apart, facing each other. The dialogue that ensued is set down here, as in my treatise *On Free Will*, without the phrases "I said" and "he said," in order that those who read it may think not that they are reading an author,

---

[10] Saint Thomas Aquinas, who insists on special status for the religious, writes: "It is better and more meritorious to do one and the same deed with a vow than without...; the works of the...moral virtues...are better and more meritorious, if they be done in fulfilment of a vow, since thus they belong to the divine worship, being like sacrifices to God." *Summa Theologica*, II², Question 88: "Of Vows," trans. Fathers of the English Dominican Province (London: Burns Oates and Washbourne, 1922), 116. The characters laugh at the Friar's words "with" and "without a cowl," possibly because he unwittingly parodies the doctor's phrase "with" and "without a vow," or because he reminds his interlocutors of the Latin proverb *Cucullus non facit monachum* ("The cowl does not make the monk").

but that they are watching and listening to two disputants.[11] So, after we were seated and while everyone paid attention in silence, I began to speak, addressing myself to the Friar.

III

LAURENTIUS: In order to remove all trace of ambiguity from our discussion, I ask, first of all, for a clarification. You were saying that although you and our friend Paulus may lead similar lives, you will receive a greater reward from God. Does this mean that although two persons may not differ at all with respect to the nature of their minds and bodies, and even though the same external things that befall mankind await both of them, and both of their lives are engaged in the same activities, yet a greater gift from God is owing to him who professes your sect (which you call "religion" [*religio*], and hence you call yourselves "religious") than to him who has not professed, nor wishes to profess, any sect, neither yours nor that of the monks nor any other?

FRIAR: Before I can answer you on this point, you make me wonder at your manner of speaking. You think that our Rule should be called a "sect" and not a "religious order" and that we should not be called "religious," as though either we are not religious or certain other persons are religious. Thereby you wish to call into question not only the dignity of our profession, which constitutes the subject of our discussion, but indeed the name itself and to strip us of our title, a long established one by now, and to disgrace us with another shameful one. Consequently you are more insulting to us than Paulus was, for he said ours is a religious order, not a sect.

LAURENTIUS: It was not my purpose to quarrel over words, especially since we have established another topic for our debate, or to divert our discussion into a different channel. But since you bid me to account for this, I shall answer you. When I engage in disputations in the company of learned men like those here

---

[11] Precedents for this justification of the use of direct dialogue can be found in Plato, *Theaetetus*, 143c; Cicero, *De amicitia* (*On Friendship*), I.3, and Petrarch, *Secret*, Preface. Valla adopts the same method in his dialogue *On Free Will*, trans. Trinkaus, 157.

present, I am not in the habit of using words that are approved by the masses rather than by experts, without providing some preliminary explanation or statement. Otherwise it would seem that, in adopting them, I accept them, and thus I could be refuted on the grounds of the terminology I use, as we see happens in judicial trials. I could cite examples of this if I were not afraid of dwelling too long on such a trivial matter. Indeed one should not only speak with precision out of mere necessity, as I have had to do now, but also for the sake of elegance. To treat only of your vocabulary, should I say, according to your usage,[12] *observantia* [CL "divine worship," ML "religious order," in the fifteenth century "a reform movement in convents involving strict adherence to original principles"] instead of *observatio* [CL "observance"]; *guardianus* [ML of Germanic origin "warden"] instead of *custos* [CL "guard"]; *claustrum* [CL "lock," ML "cloister"] instead of *atrium* [CL "courtyard"] or *porticus* [CL "colonnade"]; *ecclesia* [CL "assembly of the people," ML "church"] instead of *templum* [CL "temple"]; *sacristia* [ML "sacristy"] instead of *sacrarium* [CL "sacristy"]; *libraria* [CL "bookstore," ML "library"] instead of *byblioteca* [CL "library"]; *stola* [CL "garment worn by women," ML "stole worn by priests"] instead of *vitta* [CL "band worn by priests"]; *indulgentia* [CL "gentleness," ML "remission of sins"] instead of *venia* [CL "pardon"]; *confessor* [CL "martyr," ML "confessor"] for the person who hears the confessions of sinners; *antiphana* instead of *antiphóna* [ML of Greek origin "responsive chant"], a word which you friars corrupt both in spelling and pronunciation, and so on?

---

[12] In the last instance cited Valla points to an error in pronunciation and spelling, but his list contains principally Mediaeval Latin words, many of which are ecclesiastical terms, together with their equivalents in Classical Latin. Although he is a purist, Valla does accept more recent terms, especially when discussing religious matters, and he does fashion new Latin phrases himself when necessary (e.g. *iuraverunt in horum manibus* "swore before them" [II], and *silentium attentionemque praestantibus* "paid attention in silence" [II], which appear to be Italianisms). Some of the words listed here, along with other words examined in the work, are defined in his treatise on *The Elegance of the Latin Language* and elsewhere.

The abbreviations CL and ML used here and throughout stand respectively for Classical Latin and Mediaeval Latin.

IV
On the Name "Religious"

Nevertheless, as for your wondering at my having preferred to say "sect" instead of "religious order," you should know that I have been concerned not only with the question of elegant expression, but also with its propriety. Since I do not think, as you do, that so much store should be set by your way of life, it seemed excessive that you should ascribe such a sacred and venerable name (*religio*) to it. If this were not the case, there would be nothing for us to debate. For, if you friars alone are religious, one will have to concede that you are the best of all men. That this is not so, as I believe, is what I shall be discussing. First, therefore, I shall comment briefly on the two terms that you have asked me to explain.

The term *sect* is used properly in connection with philosophers although there were sects even in the field of rhetoric among the followers of Theodorus and Apollodorus.[13] They can be found in law and in other disciplines as well. Sects, which in Greek are called αιρέσεις [*hairéseis*] are different ways of teaching, acquiring, and practising wisdom. For the Stoics think and live in one manner, the Cyrenaics in another, the Peripatetics, Academics, and the rest in different ways. You too do something similar, and not just because some of you are monks and some friars, some hermits and some spiritual brethren,[14] but also because there are thou-

---

[13] Valla adapts the following passage from Quintilian, III.i.17–18: "the rhetoricians who attracted the most enthusiastic following were Apollodorus of Pergamus, who was the instructor of Augustus Caesar..., and Theodorus of Gadara, who preferred to be called Theodorus of Rhodes: it is said that Tiberius Caesar during his retirement in that island was a constant attendant at his lectures. These rhetoricians taught different systems, and two schools have arisen known as the Apollodoreans and the Theodoreans, these names being modelled on the fashion of nomenclature in vogue with certain schools of philosophy" (1:379).

[14] The term *agapetae*, translated here as "spiritual brethren," designated members of the clergy who in Roman times lived together with devout virgins in "spiritual" communion. Although *agapetae* can refer to the women themselves (Radetti interprets it so), the context would seem to indicate that Valla is listing various types of brothers. See G.W.H. Lampe, *A Patristic Greek Lexicon* (Oxford: Clarendon, 1961), 9. Lampe's references include Saint Gregory

sands of such individual groups, as the variety of the habits you
wear indicates. Sometimes I laugh, sometimes I become angry
when I see such vastly diverse attire on display throughout the city.
Indeed, you could scarcely find more types and colours among the
uniforms of the military. Therefore if the philosophers themselves
have termed their different ways of thinking and living "sects," you
must not be surprised if I too call those varying styles of life of yours
"sects." Nevertheless I am not concerned whether you accept this
term or not, nor am I discussing what name ought to be bestowed
on you, but I do question the name already given you, that is,
whether you should be called "religious," which was the second
part of my argument.

On this subject, then, let me continue with the comparison with
philosophers. These thinkers are insufferable when they claim for
themselves exclusively the appellation "seekers of wisdom" and
refuse to share it with any others, whether they be legislators,
illustrious senators, supreme orators, or most just sovereigns.[15]
Nevertheless, cities were governed through the wisdom of such
persons both before and after the appearance of philosophers.
Similarly who can put up with you when you state that none save
yourselves are religious, not priests, popes, or anyone else? It is a
claim that makes you look not merely presumptuous on your own
account, but also insolent toward all others. For what more lavish
praise can I receive, or, on the other hand, what more severe
reproof, than to be called "religious" or "irreligious"? Now, what
does it mean to be religious, if not to be a Christian, and indeed a
true Christian? I am not referring to the sense in which tombs are
called "religious" [i.e. "holy"] and judges and other persons are said
to be "religious" [i.e. "scrupulous"].[16] I am talking now of divinely-

Nazianzen's *Epigrammata*, II.ii.10 ("In agapetos") in *Patrologia Graeca*, ed. J.-P.
Migne, vol. 38, col. 86.

[15] The same complaint is lodged by Quintilian, I.Preface.14.

[16] In his treatise on the Latin language, 1:21 (*Opera*, 1:28), Valla explains that
a religious man is one who loves religion whereas tombs and monuments are
religious in the sense that they contain religion. The religious man is one who
adores; religious objects, instead, are adored.

Cf. Saint Thomas's definition of religion: "Although the name of 'religious'
may be given to all in general who worship God, yet in a special way religious
are those who consecrate their whole life to the Divine worship, by withdrawing

inspired religion. Although there are many religions, yet those that are false are not termed "religions," but are considered and called "superstitions," at least by those who are acquainted with true religion. True religion itself should actually be designated simply "religion" without the attribute "true" and, moreover, without the qualification "of Christ," since religion and faith are one and the same, as is a religious and a faithful person. For I describe as "faithful" not the person who is like a dead man without works,[17] but one who is active and can truly be called a Christian. As James says:

> If any man among you seem to be religious, and bridleth not his tongue, but deceiveth his own heart, this man's religion is vain. Pure religion and undefiled before God and the Father is this, To visit the fatherless and widows in their affliction, and to keep himself unspotted from the world. (James 1:26–27)

Therefore when you judge only yourselves to be religious, because you have made a religious profession, whereas you deny that others are religious, are you not indicating that you alone are Christians, you alone are good, pure and untainted, and thus you condemn and disdain others and cast them down into Tartarus? And which others? Precisely those who have already been and, I hope, are still to be placed in the category of saints. Therefore, I did not act ungenerously toward you when I hesitated to call you "religious," seeing that many others, who have not professed your "sect" or "Rule," must be called religious since they live the purest of lives, whereas many of you can not be called religious, since you live defiled lives.

FRIAR: There are arguments I could adduce in answer to your speech. However, since it was I who began to deviate from the topic we agreed to discuss, it is up to me to have us return to it, rather than stray farther from it. I can do this all the more readily since you have not positively declared that our way of living is to be defined as a "sect," nor have you completely denied that it

---

from human affairs" (*Summa*, II[2], Q. 81: "Of Religion," 9).

[17] "For as the body without the spirit is dead, so faith without works is dead also" (James 2:26).

can be called "religion." Now let us proceed on the path by which we started.

LAURENTIUS: Then answer the questions I asked. Do you recall what they were?

FRIAR: Why should I not remember them since both you and I are saying the same thing? That is, all else being equal, we who have professed religion acquire more merit than others who perform the same actions in their lives. For example, I am more meritorious than you, even though we deem ourselves to be very similar in spirit, body, conduct, and in all else, except for this one thing.

LAURENTIUS: That is precisely the point. We can not be similar at all, since we differ in opinion so radically.

FRIAR: If you had professed religion, you would share my opinion.

LAURENTIUS: That may be so, but before making your profession you did not think as I do.

FRIAR: I am older than you and I was not consecrated in this Order which I am defending until I was your age. Who can be sure that you might not follow the same course?

LAURENTIUS: Before you professed religion did you ever engage in a debate with friars and monks, questioning them about their way of life?

FRIAR: No.

LAURENTIUS: But this is what I am doing. Consequently I will never profess religion.

FRIAR: And what if that were to occur as a result of today's discussion'?

LAURENTIUS: It could be. But the issue itself is badly formulated.

FRIAR: Why?

V

Whether the Manner of Living of Those Who Have Professed Religion and Those Who Have Not Is the Same

LAURENTIUS: How can we be equal with respect to our manner of living when we lead lives that are so different? You are bound to poverty, chastity, and obedience while I am not. Thus, your behaviour differs from mine, and neither of us has anything in common with the other. It is as though you were a good painter and I a good architect. No comparison between the two is possible, and it would be very foolish to declare one superior to the other, especially if each is perfect in his kind.

FRIAR: Suppose that, being equal in everything else, we differ in these things only.

LAURENTIUS: But this amounts, so to speak, to praising you friars for architecture too, and not praising us laymen even for painting. You wish to defeat us with those three virtues, but you certainly must not be allowed to do so, since you can be surpassed by us in qualities that are different from those. It is a virtue to endure poverty, but also to distribute wealth. Chastity is good, but so is marriage. Obedience is a virtue, but so is ruling wisely. Thus some persons possess the latter qualities, some the former; no one possesses both.

FRIAR: You may have virtues that are different from ours, but they are by no means commensurate with ours, since we have taken vows.

LAURENTIUS: The question will be reversed then.

FRIAR: How is that?

LAURENTIUS: We were investigating whether you and I deserve the same reward for the same deeds. As things stand, our conduct can not be the same. What will the subject of our debate be then?

FRIAR: Let us modify it thus, if it seems appropriate: between two persons who live most holy lives, like you and me, I am more deserving by the mere fact that I have pronounced vows. For example, even if the rest of our virtues are different in kind, they can be equal in magnitude.

LAURENTIUS: I must confess to you already that you are saying an astonishing thing. Certainly no one who recalls the holiest of men, already enthroned in the Kingdom of Heaven, will agree with you. Why do you think that professing vows is so efficacious?

FRIAR: For three reasons, as far as I can recall or think. The first is that we promise to observe the following three rules at all times and in all places: to obey our superiors, to live in poverty and in chastity. The second is that we bind ourselves by the vow, from which we are not allowed to retreat. The third is that, just as a more severe punishment awaits us if we sin, so there will be a more generous reward if we refrain from sin. Indeed one can see that other men do not wish to undertake these things, either because they are reluctant to do without human goods, or because they fear the harsher penalty they will receive from God if they break their promise. This is why those who profess religion deserve praise for their magnanimity in facing these difficulties and for their fortitude in enduring them.

LAURENTIUS: The degree of magnanimity and fortitude involved will be demonstrated by the act of profession itself and by our discussion of it. Before responding to the arguments you have adduced in your defence, let us examine whether your distinction has been made correctly. It seems to me that you wanted to embellish your arguments and even frighten me with their multiplicity, like a serpent who thrusts out a single tongue that has the semblance of three. For what you stated in the first part, that is, the fact that you have promised obedience, poverty, and chastity, is a single proposition, not three separate ones. Secondly, to take a vow is more or less the same as confirming by swearing an oath that you will do what you have promised. Thus if I promise to accompany you on a sea voyage and I confirm it by swearing, I am granting you not two things, the accompanying and the swearing, but just the accompanying.[18] And lest you have any doubts about that, I introduced the oath as a proof, as it were, and I should not have done so if you had not been doubtful of my sincerity. By making your vows to God, you ratify your pledge to observe the three rules we were speaking of, so that they will not be neglected through human inconstancy, as might be the case, if there were no bond. As to what you gave as a third reason, that is, that you have greater merit, that is a sign not a cause, an argument not a proposition, a demonstration of

---

[18] Cf. Saint Thomas's views: "he that vows something and does it, subjects himself to God more than he that only does it: for he subjects himself to God not only as to the act, but also as to the power, since in future he cannot do something else...."; "There is no parity between a vow and an oath: because by a vow we direct something to the honour of God, so that for this very reason a vow is an act of religion. On the other hand in an oath reverence for the name of God is taken in confirmation of a promise. Hence what is confirmed by oath does not, for this reason, become an act of religion, since moral acts take their species from the end"; "An oath is added to a vow, not because it is more stable, but because greater stability results from two immovable things" ("Of Oaths," 117, 143, 149).

your first point not a different kind of proof. It indicates, by means of an argument from contraries, that you deserve a greater reward if you endure the three things you promised because you would receive greater punishment if you forsook them.[19]

FRIAR: Even if, by chance, these reasons are not three in number but one, what else am I attempting to do but to make our virtue seem more important because of the vow and to prove that our reward will be greater than yours? Thus what we are investigating is by now clear and with this argument alone the whole question we are debating is resolved.

VI

Whether a Greater Reward is Due Those Whose Punishment Would Be Greater

LAURENTIUS: Well then, let us see what importance these two items—your pledge and your reward—have, which, you can not deny, you have separated incorrectly. First of all let us examine the second one, in which quite rightly you place your hope for victory. And surely, if you win this point, it would be useless for me to dispute the rest. You argue that by the very fact that, if you sin, a more severe chastisement awaits you, it follows that, if you do not sin, your rewards will be more numerous. This, you say, is the normal experience of those who have professed the religious life. Yours is a concise and ready argument indeed. But I could respond just as succinctly myself by asking whence you derive the knowledge that when you err you undergo greater punishments than the rest of us? Have you perhaps descended into Hell in a dream, unless, of course, you went there in real life as a result of sinning by breaking your word?[20] But I want to refute, wound, and lay you low with another type of weapon.

---

[19] The technical terms used here in the discussion of modes of argumentation ("distinction" [divisio], "proof" [probatio], "sign" [signum], "argument" [argumentum], "proposition" [propositio], "argument from contraries" [contrarium]) are to be found in Quintilian's treatise, especially in Book 5.

[20] The state of sin is equated to a descent into Hell in Saint Augustine, The Confessions, Book 3, and in Petrarch, Secret, Book 2.

It seems to me that, just as something is worthy of the greatest reward when it is done properly, so too it is deserving of the lightest penalty when it is badly done; on the other hand, that which merits the harshest punishment if it turns out badly, by the same token deserves a minimal prize if it does not turn out badly. For the highest reward is owing to the greatest virtue and the severest punishment to the gravest offence. Similarly, a very small reward is due the least degree of virtue and the lightest punishment is merited by the most venial of sins. Thus, if your virtue is not considerable, it does not merit a large recompense. To make this clearer, it will be necessary to support it with illustrations and weigh it, as it were, against the testimony of men and public decisions. Which, then, if I may put the question to you, is worthy of greater praise and greater reward, that is to say, which showed more virtue: the person who, at some risk to his own person, snatched his parent, who was in deadly peril from a shipwreck, for example, or from a fire, or a collapsing building, or he who saved a fellow citizen or a stranger?

FRIAR: He who saved a fellow citizen or stranger.

LAURENTIUS: I also ask: if one of the two, the son or the stranger, should neglect to save the person who, as I said, is in danger, although he is able to do so without great effort, which would be more at fault and more deserving of censure?

FRIAR: Certainly the son, and not only should he be rebuked but should also be given a very severe penalty, whereas the other does not even deserve to be reproached, let alone chastised.

LAURENTIUS You are right. And so that an authority will not be lacking in our discussion, let us recall what that old man in Quintilian says against his son: "It is not a good deed to feed [one's father], it is a crime to deny [him] this."[21] One can cite endless examples of this type: if a doctor cures or fails to cure a most serious illness; if in a terrible storm a captain arrives in port having saved the ship or if he is shipwrecked; if in war a group of young boys put an equal number of grown men to flight or flee before them; if a beautiful woman is chaste or unchaste; if, without a teacher, one becomes learned or remains ignorant. The principle is the same in the opposite case, namely, if a doctor is

---

[21] [Pseudo]-Quintilian, The Major Declamations, 5:7. Trans. L.A. Sussman (Frankfurt am Main-Bern-New York: Verlag Peter Lang, 1987), 57.

faced with a very slight disease or a captain with a calm sea; if mature men in war encounter the same number of boys; if a woman is ugly; or if one does not lack a teacher. These are all circumstances in which those who, through a virtuous action, receive the utmost praise, are also treated with leniency if in the same area they fail to do something laudable. Vice versa, those who receive most criticism if they neglect virtue, merit only the slightest commendation if they have not neglected to act virtuously.

The same can be said in your case. You friars who, if we are to believe you, are subjected to a greater penalty for your sins, are therefore rewarded for your virtuous action with a lesser prize, as I have shown, just like a physician who receives hardly any praise for curing a simple disease but, on the other hand, the sharpest reproof if he does not know how to treat it. Oh how excellent and desirable is the life of friars and monks, who are granted more meagre rewards and more abundant punishments than others! If this is so, I shall not ask with what countenance you dare to exhort others to join a similar institution, but rather what can prompt you to be able to endure such a mode of existence.

FRIAR: There you go condemning religious orders with your words, not just by saying that their activities are useless and completely unproductive, but that they exert themselves to their own detriment, since they subject themselves to graver dangers and cheat themselves of more ample rewards .

LAURENTIUS: You understand, then, that your mode of reasoning is inappropriate. It is against this that I am arguing not against your Order. I maintain that reason supports my position rather than yours. So, if you are not satisfied with my conclusion you will have to reproach yourself, not me, because you introduced this argument, and you will have to retract it, even if I were to let it stand.

FRIAR: I will certainly not retract it; on the contrary, I uphold and defend it as being true, well-founded, and evident, even though you are trying to create confusion with your discourse. Would I not receive harsher punishment than you if I were to give myself over to venereal pleasures?

LAURENTIUS: Later I shall show whether you would be sinning more or not; but now, since you want me to grant you this, I shall.

FRIAR: Then why should I not receive a greater reward too?

LAURENTIUS: Have I not already answered that this is not at all a logical consequence?

FRIAR: I can not help being extremely amazed at your words. Tell me again, do you deny that if I were to fornicate, I should be committing a more serious crime than if you were to do so?

LAURENTIUS: What do you prefer me to say? Let us concede it, then: your crime would be more serious.

FRIAR: Surely, in whatever area I were to commit a graver offence, should I not also display greater virtue?

LAURENTIUS: "You are stuck in the [same] old mud."[22] Do not expect me to agree with you on this point. Otherwise I should have to concur that a greater prize awaits you. For the same relation that obtains between virtue and reward exists between crime and punishment. Thus, when I spoke just now about rewards, I answered with regard to intrinsic merit too.

FRIAR: You are almost driving me mad with these words of yours; you belittle our virtues, practically eliminate our rewards, increase our vices, and multiply our penalties; you cast the religious orders, and in fact all the religious themselves, head-long into the mud, as you said.

LAURENTIUS: It is not so; I have simply shown what the consequence of your reasoning would be. As for what your virtues and vices or your rewards and penalties are, that is God's concern.

FRIAR: Since you are speaking of God, pray tell me, even if you do not know what it is He does in Heaven and Hell, whether you really believe that He will not honour my labours and my way of life (which is so laudable, holy, and difficult) with any special gift, but will punish me more severely if I go astray. Is He therefore more inclined to punish than to reward?

LAURENTIUS: Once again you are hoping to prove, through my admission, your case, which you are unable to defend through logical reasoning. I should certainly reveal what I think if it were appropriate at this point, but I shall wait until later, when the debate demands it. For now we are disputing not the subject itself but your train of reasoning. You are unwilling to abandon it and yet you cannot defend it. Given your behaviour, I am

---

[22] Terence, Phormio, V.2.780, in *Works*, trans. John Sargeaunt (London: William Heinemann and New York: G.P. Putnam's Sons, 1925), 89.

forced to say myself that God gives you a lesser reward and greater punishment. And so that you will not think that I am voicing absurdities and expressing ideas contrary to general belief, here is my proof: almost the same proof that I presented earlier, since it appears to me that you have forgotten it. A doctor who is unable to cure a simple disease is held to be a charlatan rather than a doctor. If he is able to, he hardly deserves the praise that is owing a doctor, since this is an easy task. On the contrary, if he restores to health a man who is hopelessly ill and given up for incurable, he is deemed to be almost a kind of god; however, should he not succeed, he will not lose his reputation as a physician, since this is a very difficult feat. You cannot deny this.

FRIAR: I do not want to, nor should I.

LAURENTIUS: It can happen, therefore, that sometimes a person deserves a large recompense if he performs a deed that is commendable, but little or no punishment if he fails to do it. On the contrary, he receives a harsh penalty if he commits a shameful act and scanty remuneration, or none at all, if he does not.

FRIAR: And so are you placing us in this second category?

LAURENTIUS: Indeed it is not I who am placing you there, but rather you yourselves.

FRIAR: I am still unable to determine what you think of us.

LAURENTIUS: It is not that I want to prove something to you; rather, I wish merely to rebut your statements.

FRIAR: I do not know whether I am proving my affirmations or not. I do know that what I am saying is true: we deserve a greater reward than others. What you maintain, namely that we are offered a greater punishment and a lesser reward than you, is very far removed from the truth.

LAURENTIUS: You are asserting what is being disputed: I assert nothing myself. Nor am I being disrespectful toward your manner of living; rather, I am refuting your reasoning. So that you will understand further and be convinced, let me say that I do not think that you deserve a smaller reward than others, but not a larger one either.

FRIAR: And what about the question of punishment?

LAURENTIUS: Let us proceed in an orderly fashion. I shall disclose my opinion at the time promised.

FRIAR: Why not now?

LAURENTIUS: Who ever asks the enemy the reasons why he has drawn up his line of battle in a certain way? Nevertheless, as a friend and not as an adversary, I have conceded one of the two points to you,[23] although I could have refused to do so.

FRIAR: But this is no concession, since it is in your power to withdraw it. In fact, the other part is also in your power. It is as though you handed over a sword by its tip, but hold on to the hilt.

LAURENTIUS: Surely I need to do this to prevent you from stabbing me with the weapon I turned over to you. Continuing, then, suppose that I also concede to you that you do not merit greater punishment.

FRIAR: We are going back to the beginning of our inquiry.

LAURENTIUS: What more do you want me to grant? You will not allow me to declare that your chastisement is greater unless I also admit that your recompense is greater; you are not happy if I say that they are both equal; if I argue that they are smaller, you will accept it even less. Are you not simply demanding that I concede the whole argument to you? As you stated, quite correctly, we have gone back to the point of departure. In fact, thus far, you have not demonstrated at all why we should believe you deserve a greater reward. This is why I ask repeatedly for what reasons you have so exalted an opinion of your religious profession.

FRIAR: Do you not see that it is because of the act of profession itself, bound by vow to observe such difficult rules?

LAURENTIUS: No, I do not, especially since you admit you have been refuted on the subject we have been debating.

VII

On Vows and Why Some People Commonly Interpret Them Incorrectly

And what you now assert is another question, namely whether religious vows in themselves have merit or not.

FRIAR: I have certainly not been refuted on the former point, especially since you are going to speak further about it. But let

---

[23] The point conceded is that of a more severe punishment.

us postpone it for a moment while we examine this second question. On this topic I cannot be brought to believe that you will have anything to urge against myself, that is to say, against mankind at large.

LAURENTIUS: You cannot be persuaded, you say? But watch with what fervour I am going to speak against you: I maintain that from the very first words you friars utter, you do not know what you are talking about at all. You employ ignorantly the term *votum* ("vow") which has two significations: according to the first, it is taken to stand for "greed" and "desire," as in Virgil: "That crop, which twice has felt the sun's heat and the frost twice, will answer at last the prayers (*votis*) of the never-satisfied farmer."[24] The second meaning is that of a promise made to God, that we shall do something to please Him, if, in return, He will first grant the favour we beg of Him, provided it is not something unjust, of course. In Virgil again we read: "and sailors ashore shall pay their *vows* (*vota*) for a safe return." If we examine the origin of the latter meaning, we find that it derives somehow from the preceding one. In fact, what we ask for by means of a vow is undoubtedly what we desire most, and thus we say: 1) *vota facio pro eo*, literally, "I make a vow for it," which means "I desire it fervently," that is, "I pray the gods that what I desire may come about"; 2) *vota suscipio* or *vota nuncupo*, on the other hand, literally "I take vows" or "I pronounce vows," means "I vow," and these vows, which are undertaken and pronounced formally, are said to be "*fulfilled*," not "vows *made*." Something similar occurs among the Greeks who call a vow εὐχή [euché], and a prayer or supplication προσευχή [proseuché].[25]

I do not wish to discuss the actual pronouncing of vows, what it consists of, and in how many ways it occurs, although it is a subject worthy of a scholar. However that so-called "vow" of yours cannot

---

[24] The two passages are from *The Georgics of Virgil*, trans. C. Day Lewis, I.47–48 and I.436 (London: J. Cape, 1951), 16, 29. Italics in these and subsequent quotations are mine.

[25] A similar distinction is made by Valla in his treatise *On Pleasure* (ed. cited in Select Bibliography), II, 32: "O immortal gods..., tell me...whether anyone has ever prayed to you to bestow the virtue upon him, or has undertaken vows (*vota suscepit*) in order to obtain it, or even asked for it (*vota fecit*)..." (222–23).

be taken to be such in either of the two accepted senses, although you would like to use it in its second meaning. This you will absolutely not be allowed to do. For what vow can we find, either in false religions or in the true one, that can be taken without the condition I mentioned? Did Jacob perhaps make an unconditional promise when, as he travelled towards Mesopotamia, he said:

> If God will be with me, and will keep me in this way that I go, and will give me bread to eat, and raiment to put on, So that I come again to my father's house in peace; then shall the Lord be my God: And this stone, which I have set for a pillar, shall be God's house: and of all that thou shalt give me I will surely give the tenth unto thee? (Genesis 28:20–22)

Did Jephthah when he said:

> If thou shalt without fail deliver the children of Ammon into mine hands, Then it shall be, that whatsoever cometh forth of the doors of my house to meet me, when I return in peace from the children of Ammon, shall surely be the Lord's, and I will offer it up for a burnt offering? (Judges 11:30–31)

And Samuel's mother when, without uttering a word out loud, she said:

> O Lord of hosts, if thou wilt indeed look on the affliction of thine handmaid, and remember me, and not forget thine handmaid, but wilt give unto thine handmaid a man child, then I will give him unto the Lord all the days of his life, and there shall no razor come upon his head? (I Samuel 1:11)

But why do I mention these examples, as if the matter were not perfectly clear? Cite a single vow that has no condition and you will have won.

FRIAR: None comes to mind now. Is our taking vows meaningless then? Or how do you define what we call a "vow"?

LAURENTIUS: What else if not a promise or an oath?

FRIAR: Why is it not also a vow? He who binds himself with a vow makes a promise.

LAURENTIUS: But not all who make promises bind themselves by a vow. You yourselves are separating the promise from the vow when you say "I promise and I vow."

FRIAR: Let us divide vows into two types, conditional and unconditional.

LAURENTIUS: You are taking refuge in the license, or rather fatuousness, of distinctions. How do you dare to call a "vow" what no man of learning has designated as such? To put it bluntly, you speak that way out of ignorance.

FRIAR: Were the many learned men, who have left books written on the subject, not allowed to speak that way and to call every promise made under oath a "vow"?

LAURENTIUS: Are you saying that they were allowed what is inadmissible? Try saying that before the Greeks, Hebrews, and ancient Latins. Let one of them rise up now and prove that all those you judge to be worthy of imitation lack preparation and knowledge. He would silence you with harsh words thus: "Oh you ignorant souls, should we allow ourselves to be guided by men rather than by God? For God separated vows from promises made under oath, when he said, through the mouth of Moses in the Book of Numbers:

> If a man vow a vow unto the Lord, or swear an oath to bind his soul with a bond; he shall not break his word, he shall do according to all that proceedeth out of his mouth. If a woman also vow a vow unto the Lord, and bind herself by a bond, being in her father's house in her youth; And her father hear her vow, and her bond wherewith she hath bound her soul, and her father shall hold his peace at her: then all her vows shall stand, and every bond wherewith she hath bound her soul shall stand. But if her father disallow her in the day that he heareth; [both] her vows [and] her bonds wherewith she hath bound her soul, shall [be void]. (Numbers 30:2–5)

You see how God distinguishes between vows and oaths, implying that they differ from each other. If this were not the case, He would have been content to say 'vow' and this term could have signified oaths too, although in vows it is not necessary to swear an oath, as the previous examples clearly demonstrate. And yet what better proof of this can be had than by examining the terms, both where the form of the discourse is conjunctive, as in '[both] her vows [and] her bonds...shall [be void]', and where it is disjunctive, as in 'If a man vow a vow unto the Lord, or swear an oath to bind his soul with a bond.' Consequently, it is one thing for a person to take a vow, another for a person to bind himself by an oath. Now, what is an oath? Undoubtedly, it is a promise accompanied by swearing. In fact in the same passage, we read: '[both] her vows [and] her bonds...shall [be void], and the Lord shall forgive her, because her father disallowed her' (30:5), and 'If a man vow a vow unto the Lord, or swear an oath to bind his soul with a bond; he shall not break his word, he shall do according to all that proceedeth out of his mouth.' Thus both the vow and the oath must be promises." If one of those ancients were to come back to life, this is how he would reply to you: "What?" someone may say, "Is a promise that is made to God not valid without a vow and an oath?" This is not the time to discuss this. Suffice it to have said that a promise can be made valid either through a vow or through an oath.

FRIAR: Now I have caught you and I shall hold you on this point; namely, that our promise is made valid by means of an oath.

LAURENTIUS: I am not denying that. I concede that you friars take an oath or make a promise; I do not concede that it is a vow.

FRIAR: I am not asking you to concede this. If the oath has to be valid, and not be rendered invalid in any way, that is, if it has to be observed and fulfilled through deeds, so that we shall not be liable to punishments if this were not the case, then surely those who have bound themselves with an oath deserve recompense and reward.

LAURENTIUS: To this argument, on which you so greatly rely, I have already replied earlier when I said that if I promise to accompany you on a sea voyage and I confirm it by swearing an oath, I am doing you one favour, not two. Let me add this demonstration too: if the pledge to observe the three rules is binding, what is the advantage of swearing? If, however, it is not binding, you have not promised anything.

FRIAR: On the contrary, it is indeed valid, but the oath makes it even more so.

LAURENTIUS: I do not see what oaths have to do with it or how they can make a promise more binding. Who can cure and make healthier that which is healthy, or fuller what is full, or more perfect that which is perfect? An oath does not make a vow perfect or more perfect. Therefore it truly seems that you add the oath, admitting, as it were, that the promise is insufficient in itself, and so you use this medicine as though there were some latent disease to be treated. This usually happens when we have to deal with men who have little confidence in us, that is, who fear we shall deceive them. We insert an oath so that at least we shall appear to be God-fearing. But when we deal with God, swearing is superfluous. We do not transact with Him as we do with men, especially ever since the Son of God enlightened the world with His coming. Give heed to what He commands us to do in this matter, with His eternal words:

> ye have heard that it hath been said by them of old time, Thou shalt not forswear thyself, but shalt perform unto the Lord thine oaths: But I say unto you, Swear not at all; neither by heaven; for it is God's throne: Nor by the earth; for it is his footstool: neither by Jerusalem; for it is the city of the great King. Neither shalt thou swear by thy head, because thou canst not make one hair white or black. But let your communication be, Yea, yea; Nay, nay; for whatsoever is more than these cometh of evil. (Matthew 5:33–37)

And James, the Lord's disciple, recalling His words, says: "Above all things, my brethren, swear not, neither by heaven, neither by the earth, neither by any other oath: but let your yea be yea; and your nay, nay; lest ye fall into condemnation" (James 5:12).

Oh, what great force your oath has, which is forbidden by God Himself! And then you say that for this reason you friars have greater merit, you deserve greater reward, you offer more to God than the rest do, you who do not know how to deal with God and how much reverence He deserves. Thus I think that someone who, for example, vows to clothe ten poor persons, if his son returns home safely, cannot retract his vow, not even in the same instant that he makes it. This is understood from the words of God which firmly bind a man to his vow at the very moment that he pronounces it; they leave no room for a recantation. I do not say, as some do, that even if the son does not return, the clothes must be donated anyway, since he is not obliged to give them until after his son's return.[26] I do say though that the vow cannot be withdrawn for any other cause. For how unfair would it be if, when I have received nothing from you, and you have not done anything for me, I cannot revoke my promise?—except for the reason that, with God, one must act in a scrupulous and dutiful

---

[26] According to Saint Thomas ("Of Vows," art. 3), vows to God must be fulfilled and, furthermore, as soon as possible. No conditions are attached.

manner and with reverence. You friars do not do this: you deem your first promise insufficient unless you add an oath.

FRIAR: Pray, tell me, do you think we should make our religious profession without pronouncing vows or swearing an oath?

LAURENTIUS: Why not?

FRIAR: And would it be valid?

LAURENTIUS: Did you not say yourself it was valid, but rendered more valid through an oath?

FRIAR: Yes. But who would consider this to be a an act of profession?

LAURENTIUS: Your evil habits are the cause.

FRIAR: Does Saint Paul not say: "not only in the sight of the Lord, but also in the sight of all men" (cf. Romans 12:17 and II Corinthians 8:21)? Therefore we must make some concession to the opinion of men too.

LAURENTIUS: Provided it is morally right to do so. He says, in fact: "Provide things honest not only in the sight of the Lord, but also in the sight of all men."

FRIAR: More precisely, in the sight of God.

LAURENTIUS: In what way?

FRIAR: In that I make the promise more valid.

LAURENTIUS: You are going back to the same point.

FRIAR: More valid, I say, because I desire to be bound by a greater risk.

LAURENTIUS: Why?

FRIAR: So that a greater reward will follow.

LAURENTIUS: We discussed this before and we shall be exploring it further. Nevertheless, as a result of this, does your promise become more extensive? In your act of profession do you pledge more than those three things—poverty, obedience, and chastity even if you guarantee them with a vow, or is it that you observe more than these three precepts for the rest of your lives?

FRIAR: Surely nothing more.

LAURENTIUS: Well then, why do we not remove the oath, the vow, and so on, and examine the promise contained in your profession, from which you derive all your merit, to determine whether you who are restricted by this triple chain do something wiser, holier, and more moral than others who prefer to be free of this chain?

VIII

On Making a Religious Profession

FRIAR: Let us do so, since earlier your speech deceived me with I know not what wiles. Anyway the point is such that if you do not resolve it, you will labour in vain over the rest, which you think you have accounted for. And you will not be able to settle it unless you subvert the life and Rule of the members of religious orders—a rule of life that has been approved for so many centuries and by all people—thereby contradicting not only the saints, but even God.

LAURENTIUS: Be careful not to think or say that I have tricked you. Why should I? So that you will understand better, listen to what I want to impart to you in all sincerity and benevolence, and learn from me once and for all what your religious profession means. A religious profession is not a vow (*votum*) but a devotion (*devotio*). And a devotion, to put it briefly, is like a consecration (*dicare*) or dedication. Virgil says: "I will link [her] to thee in sure wedlock, making her thine (*dicabo*)" and "To you and [King] Latinus, have I *devoted* (*devovi*) this life."[27] To come to the defence of you friars, moreover, with my usual benevolence, let me add that sometimes pronouncing a vow (*vovere*) has the significance of consecrating (*devovere*) just as, in the same author, Camilla's father speaks thus to Diana: "[this child] I vow to thy service, I her father," that is, "to you, oh Goddess, I devote, consecrate and dedicate her." You carry out a similar act when you make your profession.

How could you say I have deceived you? Why do you not try to frighten me as well? As far as I can tell, you want me to abandon my cause out of cowardice, but there is no reason for you to think you can instil fear in me. I am not debating this with the purpose of destroying you. I am simply stating that you friars are not better

---

[27] The three quotations are from Virgil's *Aeneid*, I.73; Xl.440–42; Xl.558, trans. H. Rushton Fairclough (London: William Heinemann and Cambridge, MA: Harvard UP, 1935), 1:247; 2:265, 273. In Valla's text, the second passage reads *rex* ("king") instead of *socerus* ("father-in-law"). Saint Thomas too (e.g. Q. 82: "Of Devotion") deals with the special dedication to God signified by the verb *devovere*.

than other men; for they are equal to you in conduct and morality. And since you have wanted to arouse the hostility of those present against me, I shall have you know that, on the contrary, there have been greater individuals among those who have not professed religion than among those who have. To strike you down and lay you low with a single blow even before the duel begins, I assert (and you will have to admit it too) that they would not have been better human beings if they had made the three promises you make. And these were the most holy of men, who lived both before and after the coming of Christ: Joshua, Elijah, Isaiah, Jeremiah, Jonah, Peter, Andrew, James, John, Paul, and others. So why should I care about your religious profession if I can rise to the height of perfection without it?

FRIAR: And do obedience, poverty, and chastity not count at all?

LAURENTIUS: Certainly they do, but also outside of the religious profession. In truth those rules are not necessary for everyone.

FRIAR: In any case you do not deny that a religious profession is useful?

LAURENTIUS: I have already conceded it and, as I declared, I am not trying to undermine the Rule of your life.

FRIAR: If you concede our Rule is beneficial to men's conduct, why can that way of life not be considered superior which is graced by religious vows?

LAURENTIUS: Fire makes food more pleasant and wholesome; there are, however, many foods that are more delightful and healthful when eaten without being cooked; many of the latter variety are indeed even more pleasant and healthful. And so it is with modes of living: some are more advantageous, so to speak, if they are cooked, others if they are raw.[28]

FRIAR: Certainly ours is such that none could be more perfect.

LAURENTIUS: Indeed I should not want to detract in any way from your reputation. I am quite convinced, however, that another way of life can be just as perfect.

---

[28] In an unusual adaptation of alimentary imagery, traditionally called upon to describe intellectual and spiritual nourishment (see Ernst Robert Curtius, *European Literature and the Latin Middle Ages*, trans. W.R. Trask (rpt. New York: Harper and Row, 1963), 134–36), Valla likens the life of the religious to cooked food and the life of devout laymen to raw food.

FRIAR: So can the obligation in itself offer us no advantage? Have we promised obedience, poverty, and chastity in vain? Shall we receive no greater reward than we should have obtained had we led the same life without making pledges and, to use your phrase, if we were not consecrated, dedicated, and devoted to God?

LAURENTIUS: It probably does provide an advantage and a considerable one, but definitely not that of obtaining a greater recompense. But more about this later. First we must consider what is the nature of the three things you promise, so that their ends and advantages are made manifest.

FRIAR: That is a good idea.

LAURENTIUS: With which one do you wish me to begin?

FRIAR: With obedience, by means of which we renounce freedom, which is naturally dear not only to humans but also to birds and beasts.

LAURENTIUS: You are consistent, for, as you were speaking, you always placed this first. Do you want me to follow the same sequence you have established?

FRIAR: Yes, since I usually accept in others what I approve in myself.

LAURENTIUS: And I judge it fitting to adhere to it, moreover, so that you will not think that I am perhaps acting in bad faith with you.

FRIAR: And, if I must confess, I want you to do it for this reason too.

IX

On Obedience

LAURENTIUS: Now what is it you call "obedience"? For my part, the origin of the term is clear. It derives from *oboedio* ("I obey") which comes from *obaudio* [*ob* "towards" plus *audio* "I hear"]. Its meaning is: "I heed what is said," or "I obey," "I submit," "I gratify," or "I comply" (*obsequor*) from which one derives the noun "compliance" (*obsequium*). But I find that the term often stands for a shameful servility, as in Cicero's phrase, "if slavery means, as it does mean, the obedience of a broken and abject spirit that has no volition of its own," and, again: "[But] so long as he is subservient to [unseemliness and turpitude], he will be altogether unworthy to be deemed not merely a commander but even a free man."[29] Now, I ask you,

---

[29] Cicero, *Paradoxa Stoicorum* (*The Paradoxes of the Stoics*), V.i.35; V.i.33, in

what type of obedience do you mean? Not the one that refers to shameful things that are far removed from virtue, I surmise, but those that you believe are pleasing to God.

FRIAR: Yes. Otherwise we should be committing ourselves to obeying the devil. In fact, we promise to follow only the honest and holy orders of our superiors.

LAURENTIUS: Did you not promise God already, when you were given baptismal rites, that you would live an honourable and holy life and obey all His commands? What is the meaning of this second promise? Why do you promise men what you have already promised God? How can you give what you have already given?

FRIAR: I am not going back on my word. I am not offering to man what I already gave to God, nor am I promising a second time to God what I have already promised. Rather, I am transferring from myself to another person the authority over certain freedoms I had power over, even while serving God—matters like dress, food, movement, activities, reclining, sleeping, staying awake, and, finally, speaking. Those who have experienced it know how much patience this requires, but you too can imagine it.

LAURENTIUS: To you these things seem onerous and unbearable; to me they seem to be of no importance.

FRIAR: How can that be?

LAURENTIUS: Indeed which person, if he recalls that he is a soldier of Christ,[30] fails to impose even greater tasks than these on himself?

FRIAR: But it is more meritorious to do these things under the authority of someone else rather than on one's own.

LAURENTIUS: Beware lest it be *less* meritorious,[31] since it is harder to coerce ourselves into obeying the commands human weak-

---

Cicero in Twenty-Eight Volumes, trans. H. Rackham (Cambridge, MA: Harvard UP, 1977), 4:287, 285.

[30] "Thou therefore endure hardness, as a good soldier of Jesus Christ" (Paul, II Timothy 2:3).

[31] Many Christian writers debated the question whether it was better to serve God spontaneously or through a religious profession. In his *Refutation of the Pernicious Teaching of Those Who Would Deter Men from Entering Religious Life*, Saint Thomas rejects the view, expressed by Saint Prosper of Aquitaine (actually Julian Pomerius) in the fifth century, for one, that a good work loses

ness shuns than to execute them under order, all the more so because in the first case we play two roles, that of commanding and that of obeying. Do you think the tests Saint Paul imposed on himself were easy?[32] If you friars deem your condition more burdensome, be careful not to make us suspect that you serve God out of endurance rather than out of willingness.[33] I shall pass over in silence the fact that nobody orders you to consider it indulgence to eat cooked foods and I shall not mention that your way of life is really not so unbearable. I will say, though, that if you do only what you are commanded, you are by no means on a par with those who, while still preserving their freedom, "wandered about in sheepskins and goatskins; being destitute, afflicted, tormented; (Of whom the world was not worthy:) they wandered in deserts, and in mountains, and in dens and caves of the earth" (Hebrews 11:37-38).

But so that you will not think "I am flying [too] high,"[34] I shall leave the saints aside and get to the point, whether it is better to promise to obey. Are those who cannot submit to obedience, like kings and popes and many others, in any way deprived of this blessing? And, not to mention others, are your superiors subject to obedience?

FRIAR: Not in the least.

LAURENTIUS: And are they less meritorious for this reason?

FRIAR: No.

LAURENTIUS: Consider whether perhaps they are more so. Therefore those who are unrestrained by this law of obedience can

---

merit in proportion to the necessity for its performance (*The Contemplative Life*, II.24).

Aristotle too points out in his *Nicomachean Ethics* (III.1), that praise and blame are bestowed on passions and actions that are voluntary; only pardon and pity can be shown for involuntary acts.

[32] For example, "I *am* more; in labours more abundant, in stripes above measure, in prisons more frequent, in deaths oft" (II Corinthians 11:23).

[33] "Every man according as he purposeth in his heart, so let him give; not grudgingly, or of necessity: for God loveth a cheerful giver" (II Corinthians 9:7).

[34] The phrase is taken from Virgil, *Aeneid*, XI.751, as Cortesi has pointed out (47n). Used in a literal sense in Virgil, it has a figurative meaning in Valla, however.

have just as much merit. Now try saying that obedience is such a great thing!

FRIAR: But our superiors possess their own kind of excellence in commanding well; we have ours by obeying properly.

LAURENTIUS: Is there then no middle road between having servants and being servants? And since we cannot have authority over others, is it preferable to be willingly submissive? Not everyone is a ruler, nor is everyone a slave; not all are teachers, nor are all pupils. But neither do those in an intermediate position occupy a lower station. Just as it is desirable to gain the status of superiors or teachers, so it is regrettable to be counted among subjects and followers and, certainly, far less dignified than to be in the middle, as I have said, and to be able to live and learn on one's own, without a governor or master. I should not dare say it, but it is a sign of a lowly and ignorant mind, lacking in self-confidence, to entrust oneself like a boy to the protection and the care of a guardian or of an instructor. For if an individual is fit to advise, teach, and guide his fellows, why should he subject himself to them, especially if, as often happens, they are incompetent and unworthy? If you wish to acknowledge the truth, you will not deny that you have often experienced this and been angered by it.

FRIAR: I do not deny it. The best and most worthy individuals must, however, be made leaders.

LAURENTIUS: You are absolutely right. Consequently you must understand that superior men should be called upon not to obey but to command; those who are inferior, to obey. All the same we must recognize that a greater remuneration is due to those who rule very well than to those who are perfect subjects. Nevertheless I shall not suggest, as I could, that we must not become the servants of men because we were redeemed at such a high price.[35] As Saint Paul himself says: "Art thou...a servant? care not for it: but if thou mayest be...free, use it rather" (I Corinthians 7:21). Therefore, that promise of yours to obey is a kind of servitude.

FRIAR: Are you condemning it then?

---

[35] "Ye are bought with a price; be not ye the servants of men" (I Corinthians 7:23).

LAURENTIUS: I do not condemn it in those who cannot attain something better. However, I should prefer to be a master of others rather than a slave or, at least, the master of myself. I grant that those who are not even capable of this should submit to others so that they can live for God.

FRIAR: But most human beings are like this.

LAURENTIUS: If so few know how to control themselves, how many can there be who know how to lead others and under whose care you can seek refuge?

FRIAR: The Rule we have professed, not other men, is our emperor and commander.

LAURENTIUS: Where then is the glory and burden of obedience you referred to? To adhere to the Rule of an Order means to obey God, not men. We laymen do this too, for no better law could be drawn up than the one derived from Christ and the apostles.

FRIAR: But we see that many men have become better through their religious profession.

LAURENTIUS: I am not so stubborn as to deny that, but it does not prove that they could not have become the same or even better in some other way. But what further light does this shed on the question of obedience, especially since you claim to be good men not only for this reason but also because of your poverty and chastity?

X

On Poverty

FRIAR: Let us go on and examine these two now and, first of all, let us hear what you think of our poverty, since we have stripped ourselves of power, possessions, and the use of wealth, not only in the present but also for the future. Wherefore the well-known commonplace can truly be applied to us: "We are...prepared [willingly] to endure exile until your victory restores our rights as citizens."[36]

---

[36] Lucan, *Pharsalia: Dramatic Episodes of the Civil Wars*, trans. Robert Graves, I.278–79 (Harmondsworth: Penguin, 1956), 33.

LAURENTIUS: Let us say that poverty, as you claim, is to live as you do. You lack nothing: food, clothing, shelter, even wine. And all this is acquired without labour. This makes poverty much easier to bear, although, as Horace says: "The man is certainly not poor who has everything that he needs."[37] Very well, let us grant that you friars are truly poor, and that your virtue is indeed great; nevertheless, it cannot be said to exceed the worth of those who have not professed poverty. If I am able to live most blamelessly with riches, why do I need to embrace poverty? Being destitute is not a virtue, nor is being wealthy a virtue.[38] For example, Abraham, Isaac, and Jacob, not to mention others, were rich. Those who are "poor in spirit" (Matthew 5:3), not in material wealth, are praised, while those who are proud in spirit are condemned, because they have all the comforts of the world or "consolations," as it is written,[39] not those who, in the midst of affluence, keep a humble spirit and do not live very differently from the poor. You see how often David, the richest of all kings, calls himself poor and needy in the Psalms.[40] What other proof do you seek? If there is no difference between the way you and I live with moderation and frugality, how can it be then that you are poor and I am rich, two conditions that could not be further apart?

FRIAR: Why do you not sell everything and give it to the poor?[41]

LAURENTIUS: Shall I sell and give away my books too? This command was given to the apostles and those who were able to debate with the foremost leaders without books, without studying and preparing ahead of time. But, as for me, I really need my books and a considerable amount of money as well to be able

---

[37] Horace, Epistle I.12 (to Iccius), v. 4 (196).

[38] Aristotle argues that even a man of virtue needs material aids in life (*Ethics* X.8). Cicero too recommends temperance in the inevitable use of money (*Of Offices*, II.16–17). Saint Thomas is consistent with this line of reasoning (see *Summa*, II², Q. 117: "Of Liberality").

[39] "But woe unto you that are rich! for ye have received your consolation" (Luke 6:24).

[40] For example, "Bow down thine ear, O Lord, hear me: for I am poor and needy" (Psalm 86 [Vulgate 85]:1).

[41] "If thou wilt be perfect, go and sell that thou hast, and give to the poor" (Matthew 19:21).

to buy numerous codices and other essentials of life.[42] What could be more perverse than to donate what is yours to beggars and then go out to beg yourself? As Saint Paul says: "For I mean not that other men be eased, and ye burdened" (II Corinthians 8:13). For not everyone can or should do hard labour and, as the same Paul said, "work...with [his] own hands" (I Corinthians 4:12). And so it is enough that I do not enjoy riches or take delight in them, and that I renounce them not materially but spiritually.

FRIAR: At this point you are refuted by your own admission, inasmuch as you grant that our life is like that of the apostles, since we have renounced wealth, both in a spiritual and in a material sense.

LAURENTIUS: Not at all. I said that I need money in order to purchase books. If you act differently and surrender it to the poor you are a fool and you do not love yourself as your neighbour.[43] "[Let] the banner over me [be] love," says Solomon (Song 2:4).[44] For you are poor if you lack the things you need, and likewise if you have the volumes that are essential to you and, giving them as a gift to others, do yourself harm. I said that money is indispensable for all the other necessities of life. You should know

---

[42] Petrarch presents a similar argument in Book II of his *Secret* as he debates with Saint Augustine. He justifies his desire for books with a quotation from Horace, *Epistle*, I.18.

[43] Valla reverses the teaching of the Gospel: "Thou shalt love thy neighbour as thyself" (Matthew 19:19).

[44] The speaker of this verse is actually a woman who describes a tryst with her lover. The banner she refers to "is perhaps the sign or verbal pledge of his love for her" according to Roland E. Murphy, *The Song of Songs. A Commentary on the Book of Canticles or The Song of Songs*, ed. S. Dean McBride, Jr. (Minneapolis: Fortress Press, 1990), 52. Citing the verb in the imperative not preterite form, Valla is following the Septuagint version of the Bible rather than the Vulgate. Christian expositors of this passage had generally interpreted the banner as a reference to Christ's love and the exhortation in particular as "the Jewish Church asking the Prophets to lead her to Christ, and...the Christian Church appealing to the Apostles and Doctors for further instruction in the divine mysteries..., or...postulants for the Religious Life requesting admission from Superiors and seeking instruction in the rule and order which they propose to follow." Marvin H. Pope, ed., *Song of Songs: A New Translation with Introduction and Commentary* (Garden City, NY: Doubleday, 1977), 377.

that when you strip yourself of your possessions, you take for yourself what belongs to others. Oh how great your poverty is: you are guaranteed food, clothing, a bed, a home, and so forth, without even risking the possibility of losing them! So, Brother, consider most carefully how much it is that you claim to have offered up to God. You relinquish uncertain things and you acquire sure ones; you give up the care of others and someone else takes care of you; you abandon all hope of obtaining riches but also all the anxiety involved; you will not have anything better, but you will not suffer anything worse either. I shall not mention the many comforts that are at your disposal, whether you are healthy or sick. All this leads to the conclusion that you have not given much more than you have received. And more than a few of you take shelter in your convents, as in an animal preserve, in order to avoid a more difficult life and, after starting out as thin doves, become fat pigeons.

FRIAR: I do not approve at all of such types of people either and I do not want you to think I am speaking of them; on the contrary, I mean those who have renounced all their belongings, even including immense wealth, that is, the greatest pleasures.

LAURENTIUS: And where would you find them? Besides, do I too not surrender supreme pleasures, since I live like you who have professed poverty?

FRIAR: But you are afraid to give up material goods out of anxiety for the future and constant care about tomorrow.[45]

LAURENTIUS: And why should I be afraid if in the convent I were protected from need, as I have shown? The reason why I do not join is that I hope to please God as much as you do without these renunciations. You must not belittle the achievements of others. Otherwise why do you not impose your way of life on kings and bid them wear a hood and sackcloth? What could be more insane? Why not enjoin it on the aristocrats and senators? It is not the external man but the inner one who pleases God. Why do you not impose your Rule on pontiffs and priests who even have the task of distributing goods and riches, as is shown by the ministry and name of "deacons" [ML *diaconus* from the Greek

---

[45] "Take therefore no thought for the morrow: for the morrow shall take thought for the things of itself" (Matthew 6:34).

διάκονος (*diákonos*) "servant," "messenger," "attendant"]? Thus that famous deacon Saint Lawrence (Laurentius), worthy to be compared to the apostles, distributed the treasures of the Church which he saw were about to be seized.[46] Even the Church possesses riches and is not condemned for owning or using them, but for tightfistedness and wastefulness in handling them. The same criterion can be applied to individuals, especially according to the quality of their person.

I must not give away everything, lest I lack what is necessary for life, not for amusement or pleasure. You have not distributed everything to charity either if you have the means to live. I must not do so, because I am a soldier and I stand "in line of battle"[47] for our religion, for the Church, even for you friars or monks, and I hope my activities do not please God less than yours do. I must not give away all my belongings so as not to fail in my duty. Suppose my parents were old and ill: should I donate my property to the needy or, on the contrary, should I toil all the harder in order to furnish those parents, in the midst of the miseries of old age, with money and goods? The same consideration applies to one's wife and children. Thus it follows that I should be acting wickedly if, having parents in such a state, I were to make my profession as a religious, and Saint Paul's judgment would rightly fall upon me: "If any provide not for his own, and specially for those of his own house, he hath denied the faith, and is worse than an infidel" (I Timothy 5:8). Suppose then that I am forced to attend to earning a living out of concern for parents in this situation. Am I in any way inferior to you? Or am I superior, precisely because I should be worse if I were to profess your Rule not for the knowledge of God but in order to

---

[46] Saint Lawrence (d. *c.* 258) was a Roman deacon at the time of Pope Sixtus II. Asked to bring forth the Church's treasure, which the Emperor Valerian intended to confiscate, he gathered together a large number of the beggars and the infirm, claiming these represented the jewels of the Church. He was condemned to a slow death on the gridiron and, according to legend, when he had been on the fire for a while, suggested to his executioners that they turn him over because one side was already cooked (see Prudentius, *Peristephanon [The Martyrs' Crowns]* Hymn II).

[47] "The orator stands...in the forefront of battle" (Quintilian, X.i.29 [4:19]). Battle imagery recurs frequently in Valla's writings, as it does in Quintilian's *Institutio.*

emulate you? Certainly Saint Paul, who says of himself "since ye seek a proof of Christ speaking in me" (II Corinthians 13:3), worked with his hands, earned and spent money,[48] unlike you who do not want to touch it, as though money were fire. Many other reasons could be cited why one should not give everything away although he who gives himself surrenders all. But suppose that I distribute everything to the poor, that I promise God I will never possess riches and that I will live in poverty forever. Does that make me a monk or a friar, that is, a member of some religious order?

FRIAR: You would not actually be a monk or a friar, but you would be like one.

LAURENTIUS: What does "being like" a monk or friar mean? The former is called thus because of his solitary life [ML monachus "monk" from the Greek μόναχος (mónachos) "one who lives alone"], the latter because of the community in which he lives [CL frater "brother"]. In truth, I am not like either of them; rather, as far as poverty is concerned, I am superior to all friars and monks. But there is no reason for me to reassure God that I will live my whole life as a pauper. "Sufficient unto the day is the evil thereof" (Matthew 6:34). How can I know what will befall me tomorrow, what I shall have to do or endure? It is more than sufficient to make this pledge: "Oh God of Heaven and earth, I promise to live in as holy a manner as I can; help me keep my resolution." For this reason neither the apostles nor the martyrs nor other holy men thought they had to resort to constraint rather than liberty.

XI

On Chastity

FRIAR: What do you mean? Did they not commit themselves to observing chastity?

---

[48] For example, "Yea, ye yourselves know, that these hands have ministered unto my necessities, and to them that were with me" (Acts 20:34); "Neither did we eat any man's bread for nought; but wrought with labour and travail night and day, that we might not be chargeable to any of you" (II Thessalonians 3:8).

LAURENTIUS: That is the other question which remains to be dealt
with. Do you want me to discuss it now?

FRIAR: Yes.

LAURENTIUS: You say they committed themselves to chastity. Why
did they do it?

FRIAR: Out of their sacred duties as priests or deacons.

LAURENTIUS: Were they not also allowed to marry? As Saint Paul
says: "Marriage is honourable...and the bed undefiled"
(Hebrews 13:4). If only we Latins too were allowed this. I fear
that it was because of us—for otherwise whose fault could it
be?—that Paul said: "Now the Spirit speaketh expressly, that in
the latter times some shall depart from the faith, giving heed to
seducing spirits, and doctrines of devils; Speaking lies in hypoc-
risy; having their conscience seared with a hot iron; Forbidding
to marry" (I Timothy 4:1–3).

FRIAR: But is chastity not better than marriage? As Saint Paul recommends: "Art thou loosed...? seek not a wife" (I Corinthians 7:27).

LAURENTIUS: "All men cannot receive this saying" (Matthew 19:11).
It is much better to be safe at the middle point than to climb to
the highest point but with the risk of falling down. Oh how I wish
that bishops, priests, and deacons were the husbands of a single
wife each, rather than being, you will pardon my language,
lovers of more than one prostitute. No one can get angry with
me except he who, conscious of his own sin, does not want to
confess it. Many of them are good, but, I am sorry to say, more
numerous are the sinful. I judge you friars somewhat more
favourably, but not much, with all due respect. But let us get back
to the point. Does the priesthood or deaconship bind us to
chastity?

FRIAR: Do you not see that, because of the reverence and dignity
of the sacrament of Holy Orders, we attend to the worship of
God with a purer mind and body?[49]

LAURENTIUS: Yet, just because of his chastity, a priest will not be
more meritorious than I am. Otherwise, women, since they
cannot be priests, would be in a position of inferiority, whereas

[49] Cf. Saint Bernardino of Siena, "Sermo XVI: De sacra religione," *Opera
omnia*, vol. 1: *Quadragesimale de christiana religione* (Quaracchi: Collegii S.
Bonaventurae, 1950), 181–203.

before God there is no distinction between Greeks and barbarians, masters and servants, men and women.[50] At one time,
indeed, not even the priests and Levites, by virtue of their office,
received anything more which would make them better than the
rest of their fellow men. But if the sacrament of the priesthood
did not make a priest's marriage more holy in ancient times, and
does not enhance his chastity nowadays either, then certainly
the religious profession does not make chastity worthy of a
greater reward.

FRIAR: Then why do we promise to abstain from all venereal acts?

LAURENTIUS: What do you mean? Do you interpret chastity in this
context as meaning abstension from all venereal acts?

FRIAR: This too.

LAURENTIUS: That is ridiculous. It is as though I had more of a right
than you to be an adulterer. In this I should be as guilty as you.

FRIAR: That is not the case. I should be much more at fault.

LAURENTIUS: It seems to me you are jesting with God when you
make such fatuous and childish pledges. It is comparable to
promising never to worship idols, never to kill a man, and,
getting more to the point, never to have intercourse with your
mother or daughter. No one can be so mad as to promise not to
perpetrate these unlawful acts after he has been baptized; he was
already obliged to avoid these crimes beforehand. I ask you:
when someone enters the priesthood does he promise God
anything else but to live in celibacy?

FRIAR: Nothing else.

LAURENTIUS: Therefore, neither do you when you make your
religious profession. But, to make the point clearer, take the case
of a deacon or priest who professes your Rule.

FRIAR: That is what I did.

LAURENTIUS: You would certainly not promise celibacy then, since
you would no longer have the possibility of getting married.
What then are you declaring, to abstain from another type of
intercourse?

FRIAR: Undoubtedly.

---

[50] "There is neither Jew nor Greek, there is neither bond nor free, there is
neither male nor female; for ye are all one in Christ Jesus" (Paul, Galatians 3:28).

LAURENTIUS: Be silent, please, be quiet. If, for the sake of chastity you have given up legitimate matrimony and "the bed unde-filed," have you not also renounced other filth too, if you had not done so earlier? Because, as I said, both priests and those who enter religious orders commit themselves only to living in celibacy. What happens if, however, occasionally a person who has professed religion fails to commit himself?

FRIAR: Why?

LAURENTIUS: You yourself admitted this just now, saying that, after you were already a deacon or priest, you took the habit. For if you had already made a vow of chastity to God you could not pronounce the vow again.

FRIAR: Am I therefore not to be punished more severely than you if I do not preserve my chastity since I belong to the priesthood and to a religious order?

LAURENTIUS: Why do you judge it to be so?

FRIAR: Because I should be breaking my word.

LAURENTIUS: That is not a good reason.

FRIAR: Not a good reason, you say?

LAURENTIUS: You have forgotten what we established earlier.

FRIAR: What did we establish?

LAURENTIUS: That only celibacy is promised.

FRIAR: That is right.

LAURENTIUS: But no priest, no deacon, no friar, no monk takes a wife, that is, abandons celibacy. Perhaps you should be pun-ished more severely because of the role you have assumed. For it is difficult to play the part of a saint, to wear the habit of the apostles, to be considered a model of upright living and a reformer of the wicked, and, finally, to be one who could be crucified to the world and the world to him.[51]

FRIAR: Am I then not to be punished more severely than you if I do not fulfill my promise?

LAURENTIUS: I shall say nothing of your having sworn the oath needlessly. But, if you are so concerned about your punishment, if, the more deserving of chastisement you are for having broken your faith, the more deserving you are of rewards for having kept

---

[51] "by [Christ] the world is crucified unto me, and I unto the world" (Paul, Galatians 6:14).

it, it follows that we laymen shall not have any recompense whatsoever since we are not subject to any danger of violating promises. This is false, since I deserve a large remuneration for the alms I have given, but no punishment for those I have not donated.

XII

A Refutation of the Three Points Together

Since I have indeed refuted every single point you made and since you are no longer dealing with single issues, it is time to respond in general terms and to show what good there is in professing religion. As you say, you run the risk of perjury and faithlessness. Let us grant that your professing was a prudent, holy, and religious act. Does your whole virtue, glory, and boastfulness lie in this? Oh, what a fine thing, worthy of being proclaimed, to have placed oneself in jeopardy of committing a single sin! Does this show that you have been more charitable than others, that you have made greater offerings to God, that you deserve to be awarded a greater recompense? Oh, how little you meditate on what you profess! Let us compare our roles, yours and mine, and with examples too, so it will become more evident that the basis of your religious profession is fear not love.

Demosthenes, who could not rid himself of the bad habit of shrugging his shoulders when he made speeches, used to practise at home with a spear hanging from the ceiling and reaching close to his shoulders, so that, if in the heat of his discourse he forgot to keep his shoulders still, the jab of the spear would be a reminder.[52] This is how he cured himself of the habit. Yet we know that there were many who rid themselves of the uncouthness of a similar gesture without having to fear a lance. Here is an example in a contrary sense: when the doctors were about to cut Marius's veins, he refused to be tied down and remained unbound as they operated on him, without even moving his leg during the treatment.[53] No one

---

[52] The story of the expedient used by the famous orator of ancient Greece Demosthenes (d. 322 B.C.) is related in Quintilian, XI.iii.130.

[53] Valla's source for this anecdote concerning the Roman consul and

had done this before him. Now, I ask, which of the two do we judge to have acted more admirably? The former controlled himself by means of the thrust of a spear, the latter without any interference. The former, so as not to resist the treatment if he were untied, insisted on having himself restrained; the latter withstood the operation without being bound. The first is praiseworthy, the second is more so. The action of the former, I grant, was safer; that of the second more hazardous.

You can be compared to the former, I to the latter. You are similar to Demosthenes, I to Marius. You have obeyed someone else, I have taken on the care of others. You have lived in poverty and chastity, I have led the same type of life. To keep to these goals you have bound yourself, I have not deemed such servitude necessary. You have acted properly out of necessity, I voluntarily; you out of fear of God, I out of love of Him. "Perfect love casteth out fear" (I John 4:18). If you had not dreaded being unable to please God in any other manner, certainly you would never have bound yourself. In fact what else induced you to make the promise, or what was the point of promising, if not the possibility that, in using your own free will, something would make you deviate from the worship of God?

This is why you will see that almost all those who join your community are evil, abominable, needy, and destitute, and who despair of being able to serve God or their own body well in any other way. Thus it is not improper to say that a convent is a refuge like that of Romulus, where all the rabble of the city and the dregs of humanity converged.[54] All those who in Latium were oppressed

---

commander Caius Marius (d. 86 B.C.) may be Cicero's *Tusculan Disputations*, II.xxii.53, and II.xv.35. In Book 2 of the treatise Cicero deals with the endurance of pain. In his *Moralia*, 202b, Plutarch too praises Marius for the fortitude he showed: "without a groan or even a contraction of his eyebrows he underwent the operation...." Plutarch adds: "But as the physician turned his attention to the other leg, Marius would not consent, saying that the cure was not worth the pain." *Plutarch's Moralia*, trans. Frank Cole Babbit (Cambridge, MA: Harvard UP and London: William Heinemann, 1961), 199–201.

[54] According to the mythical account of the founding of Rome, Romulus who, together with his twin-brother Remus, had been suckled in infancy by a she-wolf, decided to create a new city, Rome. He is said to have populated it with fugitive adventurers from other lands. In the words of one early Christian

by debts, who were slaves, destitute, greedy, and wicked, rushed there precisely so as to achieve a better way of life than they thought they could attain elsewhere. Similarly, all those who take refuge in your asylum (I am not referring to the poor now) hope to live more meritoriously in the eyes of God through the risk of faithlessness and of perjury; out of fear of licence they deprive themselves of freedom and practically impose a law upon themselves. Similarly, Alexander the Great,[55] who was spurred by an ardent desire to destroy the city of Lampsacus, was agitated when he saw his master Anaximenes coming out of the city walls, fearing that the latter's loyal prayers would force him to spare the city against his will, swore that he would not do what his master requested. But Anaximenes said: "I am asking you to destroy Lampsacus." Thus, although that most powerful king, afraid of violating his oath, sought to be compelled to do as he willed, he was forced instead to do what he had not planned.

In truth, every kind of vow, every resolution to fast, every oath, even every law (and religious profession amounts to the acceptance of a law) was devised out of fear or, frankly speaking, for the sake of the wicked. And you boast that you are magnanimous and tolerant? Are you still in doubt? Does Saint Paul not say "the law...was added because of transgressions" (Galatians 3:19)? The king bears a sword because of his evil subjects not the good ones.[56] The Hebrews lived once without laws. Did Abraham and the others who lived before the law was promulgated, Job, King Cyrus, the Queen of Sheba, and the others from the Old Testament who did not live under the law, receive a lesser reward than those who did?

---

writer: "the original lower orders assembled at Asylum—a conglomeration of the scum and dregs of society, profligates, gangsters, traitors...." Marcus Minucius Felix, *The Octavius*, trans. G.W. Clarke, ch. 25, Ancient Christian Writers, vol. 39 (New York: Newman Press, 1974), 96.

[55] This incident in the life of Alexander the Great (d. 323 B.C.), King of Macedon and conqueror of much of Asia, is told in Valerius Maximus, *Anecdotes*, VII.iii.4. Anaximenes is the rhetorician to whom is attributed the original division of rhetoric into three basic genres: judicial, deliberative and epideictic.

[56] Cf. "For rulers are not a terror to good works but to the evil....Do that which is good, and thou shalt have praise of the same....But if thou do that which is evil, be afraid; for he beareth not the sword in vain...." (Paul, Romans 13:3–4).

Definitely not; their recompense was at least equal. And, conversely, to disclose to you now what I earlier promised to reveal, if they sinned, would they have been given an equal punishment? Certainly not, but a smaller one. Then stop fussing and complaining because those who have faced fewer risks of being punished receive equal honours, and stop blaming God, so to speak, like those who grumbled among themselves because the same payment was made to the first as to the last workers.[57]

Drawing an analogy with the human condition, I ask you, does a king who leads an honest life deserve less praise among men than a commoner, because the king can sin with impunity but the private citizen cannot? Surely he deserves not less but more praise, since the virtue of self-restraint is more difficult for a monarch. And if he sins, he deserves a lighter punishment, since it is easier for a ruler than for an ordinary citizen to sin and cause harm. And so it is with divine matters. But you request approbation for having been in peril, like a soldier who demands compensation from the king because he was in danger of losing his life had he surrendered the camp treacherously to the enemy. Undoubtedly the king would reply thus: "If you did not betray the camp because of your fear of death, consider it a reward that I am not going to kill you. Be happy with your payment, as is he who did not commit treachery, not out of fear but out of love." Who does not understand this?

You professed religion in order to win eternal life; behold, what your heart longed for has now come true; you have obtained what your promise required. You owe everything to this risk: you exposed yourself to the danger of swearing an oath falsely, but through this risk you have saved yourself from ruin. You often trembled with fear, but now you rejoice. You were afraid of breaking the pact at some time. You realize though that you could not have swum to safety in any other way. I do not understand then what else you can possibly demand from God except the reward of obedience, poverty, and chastity. Dissatisfied with this, however, you insist upon being placed before all others in return for having assumed a risk. But if you take into account the risk of punishment you incur, you must also consider the hazards I face of sinning more easily, since I am not held down by the anchor of fear. As a result,

---

[57] Matthew 20:1–14

the same virtuous action is of greater consequence if performed by me than by you. I am superior to you just as Marius is superior to Demosthenes, and the king to the soldier or commoner. Indeed, I do not deny that some who have professed religion reach the stage of eliminating fear, but, certainly when they make their profession, they are not without fear. And yet, when they reach perfection, they are not dominated by the dread of faithlessness or chastisement; rather, like free and unshackled souls, they are led by the spirit of God, and live as though they had never made a promise.

Saint Paul says of those who eat and those who do not eat: "Let every man be fully persuaded in his own mind" (Romans 14:5). And so let us call it a draw and conclude that a religious profession does not make men better, just as the deaconship, priesthood, bishopric, and the papacy do not either. You are not more honest because you embraced the deaconship or the priesthood; rather, you wanted to be consecrated so as to become better. You are not greatly deserving because you have sworn an oath; rather, you took an oath in order to be greatly deserving. You are not good because you are liable to punishment, for truly you can be bad; nay, it was in order to be good that you incurred the danger of punishment. Is Saint Lawrence who was a deacon perhaps less of a saint than Pope Sixtus? I am not afraid to consider Saint Stephen, also a deacon, equal to many apostles. Is Saint Francis, who refused the priesthood, less meritorious than any of his companions or subsequent members of his Order? Is Saint Martin, who remained a catechumen, to be placed below all those who founded so many communities of friars and monks?[58] Briefly, can John the Baptist, who was

---

[58] Saint Sixtus, pope from 257 to 258, was beheaded a few days before his deacon Lawrence during the persecution of the Christians organized by the Emperor Valerian. Saint Stephen, a deacon and apologist for the Christian faith, was stoned to death in the year 367. Saint Francis of Assisi (d. 1226) rejected his family's wealth in favour of an ascetic life dedicated to the imitation of Christ's ideals and the preaching of humility, charity, and above all poverty. Not satisfied with existing monasticism he established the Order of Friars, to which the interlocutor in Valla's treatise may perhaps belong (see note 60 below). In addition to performing miracles, he is believed to have received Christ's stigmata. Saint Martin of Hungary (d. 397) is known as the "soldier saint" for he abandoned his military career to embrace a saintly life. Even though he was a catechumen, having received only the sacrament of Baptism, such was his

not a bishop or priest or a member of a religious order, be regarded as inferior to any bishop, priest, or friar? I realize that those who founded your convents were obviously induced by the desire to provide you with many advantages for a sacred life—certainly a holy and laudable cause, because of which many have won laurels from God, although not in such great numbers as you friars say.

But similar inducements have not been taken away from others, whereas the majority of you have abandoned the path of your founders. That is why for a long time now (as the ancients used to say of Apollo of Delphi, who had stopped uttering oracles)[59] you friars have ceased to perform miracles, although more than a few of these are called into question. I shall not do this since my purpose is to act as the defender, not the accuser, in this matter. I merely wanted to refute first of all the idea that you have greater merit because you are exposed to a greater danger of chastisement for your errors; secondly, the view that making a vow and promising several things by swearing an oath are the same; finally, the opinion that you friars are endowed with some prerogative and privilege because you promised obedience, poverty, and chastity.

And so that you will not think that I am your enemy, and in order to regain your good graces, I shall now sing the praises of friars. Friars are those who truly support the tottering temple of God, as you usually depict it,[60] those who by delivering sermons to the

---

reputation that he was appointed Bishop of Tours, albeit against his will. According to legend, his conversion came about when, moved at the sight of a beggar, he slashed his cloak with his sword and gave one-half of it to the mendicant.

[59] Cicero, *On Divination*, II.lvii.117, and II.lvi.116. Minucius Felix, ch. 26, speaks of the falsity of pagan oracles: "Ennius forged the replies of Pythian Apollo about Pyrrhus, for Apollo had ceased to produce verses by that stage. That wary and ambiguous oracle failed just when men started to become more sophisticated and less gullible" (99).

[60] According to his early biographers (see Thomas of Celano, *Second Life*, Bk. 1, chs. 6, 11), Saint Francis heard a voice coming from the crucifix bidding him to go and repair God's house, which was falling into ruins. Consequently he approached Pope Innocent III to ask permission to establish a new religious order with its own Rule. After their meeting the Pope dreamt that the Lateran basilica was about to fall, but that a humble friar came to support it with his shoulder. In a famous fresco by Giotto, Saint Francis holds up the Church with

people (this was formerly and ought now to be the task of bishops and priests) turn men and women away from sin, freeing them from false beliefs and leading them to piety and knowledge. In this I believe friars are very similar to the apostles. With awe-inspiring ceremonies, hymns, and songs friars arouse religion in our hearts. Friars daily compose many works on morals, virtue, and holiness (yet I wish they would write them in a more learned fashion and, as was formerly done, in the style of oratory rather than that of philosophy). With supreme wisdom friars either absolve those who confess their sins or terrify them by denying absolution. Friars send away, enlightened and encouraged, those who consult them on how to live well. Finally, the whole world is deeply indebted to friars and would be even more so if they were more moral, as I do believe they were at the beginning. I think I have said more than enough in praise of you friars. If I have expressed some criticism of you, you should accept it with equanimity, especially since I feel I have not made any false representations.

XIII

Then the Friar declared that he certainly was not irritated by what I had said, but neither would he concede victory to me in the dispute. For he wanted to reflect on the matter more carefully and resume the controversy again if he thought fit. At this point all the others announced that they had decided in my favour; Paulus said: "I agree with you, Laurentius, on all else; yet I am not satisfied with the ending, or peroration, which was not so much a praise of friars as proof of your timidity. For although it would have been logical for your speech, as it had begun, to end with an attack against friars, as you could have done most eloquently, you preferred instead to

---

one hand. Although this reference has been the basis for identifying the Friar in the dialogue as a Franciscan (see Cortesi's conjectures, xxxvii-xli), throughout the treatise Valla appears to be referring to members of religious orders in general. It may be pertinent to note, moreover, that he uses a similar metaphor in the phrase *columnae ecclesiae* ("columns of the Church") (*Elegances*, Preface in *Prosatori*, ed. Garin, 620) in reference to eloquent writers and especially the Fathers, who are called "columns of the temple of God" at the beginning of his treatise *On Free Will* (155).

conclude by praising them, so as not to arouse their animosity against you. Besides, I shall consider you very cowardly and unmanly unless you write down the debate in the order in which it was conducted, make it public as soon as possible and deliver it into the hands of the people with the title, moreover, 'On the False Name and Privilege of the Religious'."

Then I said: "Yes, I shall copy it out, but not with that terrible title, although it is perhaps an accurate one. And if a week from today, at the same time and in the same place, our Friar does not present himself and appear at the appointed date in court, so to speak,[61] not only shall I make it public, but I shall bring the work to the attention of some very learned and wise person and have it examined by him. In truth, I already have someone in mind to consult; you also indicate whom you think I should confer with." And all unanimously said that Baptista Platamon, one of the leading men of our generation, an expert in all subjects and important disciplines, ought to be my adviser. I said: "I too had chosen that very person." When all this had been said, and the Friar too had agreed, we stood up. And since he had arrived last, he was the first to depart, exchanging greetings with the rest, but he did not turn up on the appointed day. Therefore, we were enabled to deliver the work for examination to the person designated.

---

[61] Valla uses a technical legal term *vadimonium* ("the appointed hour") indicating the promise made by a defendant concerning due appearance in court. See Adolph Berger, *Encyclopedic Dictionary of Roman Law* (Philadelphia: The American Philosophical Society, 1953), 757. The word recurs in Cicero's oration in defence of Quinctius who, in a dispute over property, was accused of having resorted to delaying tactics by not appearing in court.

Selections from
The Falsely-Believed and
Forged Donation of Constantine

I, 1 Some people are offended because in the numerous books I have published, in almost every field of learning, I disagree with some great authors who have been acclaimed for a long time. They accuse me of sacrilege and audacity. Well, I wonder, what will they do, how enraged will they be against me, and how eagerly and hastily would they drag me off to torture, if they only could, now that I am writing not just against the dead but against the living too, not just against this or that individual but against a multitude of men, not merely private citizens but even public officials? And which officials? Why, even the Supreme Pontiff himself who is armed not only with a temporal sword, like kings and rulers, but with a spiritual one too, so that you can not defend yourself from being visited with excommunication, anathema, or curse, not even by seeking refuge beneath the shield of princes, so to speak....

2 ...The high priest Ananias, before the tribune that sat in judgment, gave orders that Paul, who said that he had lived according to his conscience,[1] should be struck on the mouth, and Pashur, who held similar authority, threw Jeremiah into prison for having spoken freely.[2] However, the tribune and the governor wished and were able to protect Paul against the unjust pontiff,[3] and the king did the

---

[1] Acts 23:1–2
[2] Jeremiah 20:1–2
[3] Acts 23:10, 26–35

same for Jeremiah.[4] But, in truth, if the supreme priest were to drag me away, what judge, what governor, what king, even if he wished to, would be able to rescue me?

Yet there is certainly no reason for me to be distressed and swayed from my purpose by this twofold peril. For the Supreme Pontiff is not allowed to restrain or release anyone against either human or divine law. Moreover, to sacrifice one's life in order to defend truth and justice constitutes the greatest virtue, the greatest praise, and the greatest reward. Many have run the risk of dying in order to defend their country on earth; shall I be afraid to risk death in order to reach the celestial fatherland? Indeed it is those who please God, not men, who reach Heaven.[5] So, away with trepidation, anxiety begone, fears disappear! One must defend the cause of truth, the cause of justice, the cause of God, with steadfast courage, great confidence, and undying hope. For he who has the ability to speak well should not be considered a true orator unless he also has the courage to speak.[6] Let us, then, venture to accuse whoever it is that carries out actions deserving of accusation. And let him who sins against everyone be reproached by the voice of one individual on behalf of all....

4 My purpose is not to inveigh against any person and compose Philippics[7] against him; far be this misdeed from me. Rather, I seek to eradicate error from men's minds, to remove them from vice and evil, either through warnings or reproach. I hardly dare say it, but my aim is to instruct those who, with an iron blade, will prune the Papal See, that is, Christ's vineyard, which is rife with over-abundant undergrowth, and force it to bear plentiful grapes rather than meagre wild vines.[8] As I do this, is there perhaps someone who will want

---

[4] Jeremiah 39:11–12

[5] "For do I now persuade men, or God? or do I seek to please men? for if I yet pleased men, I should not be the servant of Christ" (Paul, Galatians 1:10). Cf. I Thessalonians 2:4.

[6] "he is the orator whose task it is to speak well"; "No man will ever be the consummate orator of whom we are in quest unless he has both the knowledge and the courage to speak in accordance with the promptings of honour" (Quintilian, II.xiv.5: 1:301, and XII.ii.31 [4:399, 401]).

[7] Cicero wrote Philippics, or polemical orations, against Marc Antony. The name is derived from Demosthenes's speeches against Philip II of Macedon.

[8] "My wellbeloved hath a vineyard in a very fruitful hill; And he fenced it, and

to shut my mouth or his own ears and threaten me with the death penalty, so that I shall be silent? What should I call one who would do this, even if he is the Pope? A "good shepherd" (e.g. John 10:11), perhaps? Or a "deaf adder that stoppeth her ear: Which will not hearken to the voice of [a] charmer" (Psalm 58:4–5 [57:5–6]) but wants to strike his limbs with her poisonous sting?

II, 5 I understand that the ears of men have been waiting for a long time to hear with what crime I am about to charge the Roman Pontiffs. Surely it is a most serious crime, of either lackadaisical ignorance or enormous greed, which is a form of idolatry,[9] or the vain will to power, which is always accompanied by cruelty. In fact, for several centuries now either the popes have not understood that the donation of Constantine is a forgery and a fabrication, or they have invented it themselves, or else, as followers treading in the footsteps of their predecessors' deceit, they have defended it as being true, even while knowing it was false. Thus they have disgraced the dignity of the pontificate and the memory of the early popes, dishonoured the Christian religion and caused general confusion with massacres, destruction, and shameful actions. They say that the city of Rome, the Kingdom of Sicily and Naples, the whole of Italy, Gaul, Spain, the lands of the Germans and Britons, and, finally, all of the West belong to them. And all these things, purportedly, are contained in the pages of the donation. Are these lands then all yours, oh Supreme Pontiff? Do you intend to recover all of them? Do you plan to strip all the kings and princes in the West of their cities or compel them to pay annual taxes to you? On the contrary, I deem it to be more just if the rulers are allowed to deprive you of all the dominion you hold, since, as I shall demonstrate, that donation, from which the popes claim their rights derive, was unknown either to Pope Sylvester or to the Emperor Constantine.

---

gathered out the stones thereof, and planted it with the choicest vine, and built a tower in the midst of it, and also made a winepress therein: and he looked that it should bring forth grapes, and it brought forth wild grapes....For the vineyard of the Lord of hosts is the house of Israel...." (Isaiah 5:1–2, 7).

[9] "no whoremonger, nor unclean person, nor covetous man, who is an idolater, hath any inheritance in the kingdom of Christ and of God" (Paul, Ephesians 5:5).

6 However, before I come to the confutation of the text of the donation,[10] the only defence they have, and one that is foolish as well as false, I must go back to an earlier period for the sake of order. And, first of all, I maintain that neither Constantine nor Sylvester was able to carry out the transaction: the former had no motive to make the donation, had no right to make it, and no power to hand over his possessions to someone else; while the latter had no motive to accept the gift and had no right to do so. Secondly, even if this were not absolutely true and evident, as it is, the Pope did not receive nor did the Emperor transmit possession of what is supposed to have been donated. It always remained in the power and dominion of the Caesars. Thirdly, Constantine gave nothing to Sylvester, but rather to the previous Pope, even before he received Baptism, and those gifts were modest ones on which the Pope could barely subsist. Fourthly, it is incorrect to say that the copy of the donation is to be found in the *Decretum*[11] or that it was taken from the Life of Sylvester since it is not included either in this or in any other historical work. Moreover, it contains certain elements that are contradictory, impossible, foolish, strange, and ridiculous. I shall speak also of the supposed or paltry donation made by other Caesars and I shall add, in supernumerary argument, that even if at one time Sylvester had held title, yet, because either he himself or some successive pope was dispossessed, it can not, after such a long interval of time, be reclaimed either according to divine law or to human law. Finally, the pope's possessions could not have been won through prescription,[12] no matter how long he held them.

III, 7 And so, as for the first point (and we shall speak first of Constantine, then of Sylvester), it is not appropriate to discuss a public and, we might say, an imperial case using discourse that is

---

[10] Coleman (see Bibliography), 10–19, includes the Latin text together with an English translation of it. The donation document was published as an interpolation in Part 1, dist. xcvi, ch. 14 of the *Corpus iuris canonici*, ed. Aemilius Friedberg (Lipsiae: B. Tauchnitz, 1879), vol. 1, cols. 342–45.

[11] The *Decretum* is a synthesis of Church law compiled by Gratian, a twelfth-century Italian professor of law and moral philosophy.

[12] Active prescription, that is the claiming or reclaiming of a legal title on the basis of possession, is dealt with in *The Civil Law*. See the *Code of Justinian*, VII.xxxiii-xl, trans. S.P. Scott (New York: AMS Press, 1973). See Berger (645), for the entry on "Praescriptio longi temporis."

not more elevated than that used normally for private affairs. Thus, I am going to pretend I am delivering a speech to an assembly of kings and leaders (as in reality I am doing, since this oration of mine will come into their hands), and I shall address them as though they were present before me: "I ask you, kings and rulers (and since it is difficult for an ordinary man to imagine the mind of a king, I shall analyze your way of thinking, examine your conscience, and ask for your testimony), is there anyone among you who, had he been in Constantine's position, would have deemed it proper to donate to someone else, as a mark of generosity, the city of Rome, his place of birth, the capital of the world, the queen of all cities, the most powerful, most noble, and richest of all peoples, the conqueror of nations, sacred in her very appearance, and then retire later to the humble town of Byzantium? Would he, furthermore, have given away, together with Rome, all of Italy, which is not a province but the conqueror of other provinces? Would he have relinquished the three Gauls, the two Spains, the Germanic peoples, the Britons, all of the West? Would he have deprived himself of one of the two eyes of the Empire? I can not be led to believe that anyone in his right mind would do such a thing.

8 "What can befall you that is more desired, delightful, and pleasant than to augment your empires and kingdoms, and to extend your rule as far and wide as possible? It seems to me that you devote every care, thought, and effort, day and night, to this purpose. It is from this that you derive your chief hope for glory, it is for this that you sacrifice pleasure, face a thousand risks, and bear uncomplainingly the loss of your dear ones or of part of your own body. Indeed, I have never heard or read that any of you has been deterred from striving to increase his dominion, even if one of his eyes or hands or legs or any other part were to be cut away. And this passion, this desire for immense rule agitates and torments most intensely those who are most powerful...."

10 ...What compelling and pressing reason could there have been for him to neglect everything and display such generosity?

IV, 11 They say, because he had become a Christian. And would he therefore have given up the best part of the empire? Now that he was a Christian, had it become a crime, a shame, or a sacrilege to govern, and could political rule not be reconciled with the Christian religion?... Oh, Constantine, they say that you were led to do this out of respect for religion, as though it were more religious to give up ruling than to govern well for the protection of religion....But if you wish to show you are a Christian, that you are devout and care not only for the Church of Rome, but also for the Church of God, precisely for this reason you must act like a ruler now and fight on behalf of those who cannot and should not engage in combat, and protect with your authority those who are exposed to snares and insults....Have you become a Christian, Constantine? Then it is absolutely shameful for you to have less power now as a Christian emperor than when you were an infidel. Sovereignty is indeed a special gift from God; even pagan rulers are considered to be chosen for it by God.[13]

12 "But he had been cured of leprosy [by Pope Sylvester] and therefore it is likely that he wanted to show his gratitude and repay in greater measure what he had received," an objector might say. Really? If Naaman the Syrian, when he was cured by Elisha, simply offered a few gifts, not half of his possessions,[14] can it be that Constantine offered half of his empire? I regret having to respond to a shameless fable as though it were indisputable history. In fact this legend must have been designed on the basis of the biblical story of Naaman and Elisha....And you would have it that Constantine donated his kingdom to God...when, by so doing, he would have offended his children, humiliated his friends, neglected his relatives, harmed his country, brought sorrow upon everyone, and forgotten his own interests?

V, 13 And even if he had been capable of doing this and if he had almost been transformed into a different man, surely someone would have warned him, above all his children, relatives, and friends. Would not everyone agree that these people would have gone to the emperor immediately? You can imagine how, after hearing of Constantine's plan, they would have rushed in alarm to

---

[13] "Let every soul be subject unto the higher powers. For there is no power but of God: the powers that be are ordained of God" (Paul, Romans 13:1).

[14] Naaman, a military commander stricken with leprosy, sought aid from Elisha, a prophet of Israel and performer of miracles. After curing him, Elisha refused the offer of gifts, but his servant took money from Naaman and was then punished with leprosy himself. The story is told in II [IV] Kings 5:1–27. The biblical story, but with the omission of details on the gifts offered, was included in various mediaeval sources like the *Life* of Sylvester published in Bonino Mombrizio (cited below in note 39).

kneel before the ruler and, sighing and crying, would have pronounced this speech:

"So this is how you, father, who were once so affectionate to your children, now strip, disinherit, and disown us? We do not so much deplore the fact that you should wish to strip yourself of the best and largest part of your empire as we are surprised by it. But we complain because by conferring it on others you cause us harm and dishonour. Why is it that you defraud your children of the succession they expected to the empire which you yourself have ruled as did your father?..."

14 Unless we are of the opinion that "human qualities have been altogether uprooted from his mind,"[15] would Constantine not have been moved, if not spontaneously, then by this speech? And if he had not wanted to listen to them, would there not have been those who would have objected with words and deeds? And would the Roman Senate and People not have judged it appropriate to take action in such an important matter? Would they not have called to their aid an orator "honoured for noble character and service," as Virgil says?[16] He would have addressed the following speech to Constantine:

"Caesar,[17] even if you have forgotten your subjects and yourself to the extent that you do not wish to give your sons their inheritance, nor riches to your relatives, nor honours to your friends, nor do you wish to preserve the integrity of the Empire, nevertheless, the Senate and the People of Rome cannot forget their rights and their dignity. And in fact how can you take such liberty with the Roman Empire, which was generated not by your blood but by ours? Will you cut a single body into two parts and from one make two kingdoms, two leaders, two minds? And, so to speak, will you hand swords to two brothers who will fight over the inheritance?...What will happen if, either during your lifetime or after your death, some barbaric

---

[15] Cicero, *Laelius, On Friendship*, XIII.48, trans. J.G.F. Powell (Warminster: Aris and Phillips, 1990), 51.

[16] The phrase from Virgil's *Aeneid* (I.151), trans. H. Rushton Fairclough, 1:250, is cited by Quintilian (XII.i.27) in connection with his definition of the orator who is above all a good man.

[17] The name Caesar is used to indicate the title assumed by the Roman emperors from Augustus Caesar onward.

nations were to wage war against the part that you surrender or the part that you keep for yourself? With what military force, with what resources shall we be able to resist? If now we can hardly do it with the troops of the whole Empire, what shall we be able to do in such a case?...Generally when a kingdom is divided between two brothers the soul of the people is immediately divided and they begin to wage war among themselves rather than with the enemies from outside. Who does not realize that the same thing will happen in this empire?...

15 "...Caesar, as far as your own affairs are concerned, you will see to them; however, this matter is necessarily of concern to us no less than to you. You are mortal, but it is fitting that the Empire of the Roman people be immortal.[18] In so far as it is within our power, not just the Empire but also its honour will be immortal. **16** ...Truly, Caesar, if we had chosen you as our king, you would have limitless authority to do with the Roman Empire as you please, but not such as to diminish its majesty even in the least. Otherwise we, who might have made you king, would have the same right to force you to abdicate your sovereignty. By no means could you divide up the kingdom, alienate so many provinces, hand over the very capital of the kingdom to a lowly foreigner. We appointed a watch-dog to tend the sheepfold, but, if he prefers to behave like a wolf, either we shall drive him out or we shall kill him. Now will you, who for a long time have acted as a watch-dog in defence of the Roman sheepfold, finally, as no one before you, be transformed into a wolf? **17** ...We shall speak our minds, Caesar, if you do not wish to rule over Rome, you have sons, one of whom you could put in your place. This would accord with natural law and we would permit and request it. Otherwise we intend to defend the public grandeur and our private dignity. This insult to the Romans is no less grave than the rape of Lucretia of old, nor will we lack a Brutus who will offer himself as a leader of the people to attack Tarquin and restore freedom.[19] We

---

[18] The notion of Rome's eternity is found in Virgil's *Aeneid*, I.279: "dominion without end" (1:261); and in Livy, e.g. IV.iv.4, where Rome is said to be "a city founded for eternity" (1:269).

[19] Livy (I.lvii–lx) reports that when Sextus Tarquinius, son of Tarquin the Proud, king of Rome (534 B.C.–510 B.C.) raped Lucretia, who then took her own life, the people rebelled and, led by Brutus, deposed the king and

shall strike first those whom you appoint as our leaders and then you, just as we did with many emperors, even for less serious causes."

These words would certainly have moved Constantine, unless we consider him to be hard as a rock or a tree-trunk.[20] And if the people did not actually give the speech, it is likely that they said these words to one another or freely uttered them in rage.

VI,18 ...Let us grant, if it is possible, that neither prayers nor threats nor any other type of reasoning were effective and that Constantine still persisted and absolutely refused to abandon his decision. Could anyone have resisted being moved to approve Sylvester's oration if it had actually been delivered? It would undoubtedly have been as follows:

19 "Caesar, honourable prince and son, I can certainly not help but be delighted and flattered by your devotion, humble and generous as it is. But, somewhat mistakenly, you offer gifts to God and sacrifice victims, and I am not at all surprised by it, since you are still a recruit in the army of Christ. Just as at one time a priest was not allowed to sacrifice any animal, wild beast or bird,[21] similarly he may not now accept any gift whatsoever....Your gifts or, if you prefer, your recompense would defile and completely destroy the glory, innocence and sanctity that are mine and of all my successors.... **20** Indeed, Elisha, who had cured Naaman the Syrian of leprosy, refused to accept a reward, and so shall I, who have cured you, accept it? He refused gifts, and shall I allow kingdoms to be given me? He did not wish to dishonour the image of the prophet; and shall I dishonour the image of Christ that I carry within me? ...As

---

re-established freedom for Rome.

[20] In *Laelius, On Friendship*, Cicero includes the observation: "If you take away the mind's capacity to feel emotion, what difference is there, I do not say between an animal and a man, but between a man and a tree-trunk or a rock or anything else of that kind?" (XIII.48).

[21] "You, therefore, O bishops, are to your people priests and Levites, ministering to the holy tabernacle, the holy catholic church; who stand at the altar of the Lord your God, and offer to Him reasonable and unbloody sacrifices through Jesus the great High Priest"; "the Lord...does not permit you to sacrifice irrational creatures for sin-offerings, and purifications, and scapegoats...." *The Apostolical Constitutions*, ed. James Donaldson, Bk. 2, sec. iv, par. 25, 35 (Edinburgh: T. and T. Clark, 1870), 56, 65.

the Lord says, 'It is much more blessed to give than to receive' (Acts 20:35). **21** My case is the same or rather more to the point, since the Lord advised me with these words also: 'Heal the sick, raise the dead, cleanse the lepers, cast out devils; freely ye have received, freely give' (Matthew 10:8)....

22 "Truthfully, how will the innocence of priests possibly remain untarnished amidst riches, offices, and the administration of the affairs of the world? Have we then renounced worldly goods in order to acquire them in even greater abundance? And have we cast aside our private possessions, in order to hold public property and others' possessions? Shall the cities be ours, the tributes ours, and the taxes ours? And how will it be possible for us to call ourselves clerics if we do this? Our lot or destiny, which in Greek is termed κλῆρος (*kleros*), is the Lord;[22] and it is not an earthly lot, but a heavenly one....Heed...what Paul said:

> We brought nothing into this world, and it is certain we can carry nothing out. And having food and raiment let us be therewith content. But they that will be rich fall into temptation and a snare, and into many foolish and hurtful lusts, which drown men in destruction and perdition. For the love of money is the root of all evil: which while some coveted after, they have erred from the faith, and pierced themselves through with many sorrows. But thou, man of God, flee these things (I Timothy 6:7–11).

And, Caesar, would you order me to accept what I must avoid like poison?...

25 "Furthermore, would I not be expected to exercise the power to kill, when punishing criminals, waging wars, sacking cities, and destroying regions with sword and fire? Otherwise I could not hope to preserve what you would give me. And if I did that, would I be a priest, a pontiff, a vicar of Christ?...

---

[22] Psalm 72:26. Isidore of Seville, for example, explains that the clergy is thus named because the first priest was chosen by lot (*Etymologies*, VII.xii.1). The verse from the psalm was cited by Saint Jerome in his explanation of the term: "the clergy are so called either because they are the lot of the Lord, or else because the Lord Himself is their lot and portion." *Letter* LII, par. 5 in *The Principal Works of St. Jerome*, trans. W. H. Fremantle et al., Nicene and Post-Nicene Fathers, ser. II, vol. 6 (Oxford: James Parker and New York: Christian Literature Co., 1893), 91.

26 "Therefore, Caesar (let it be said with your permission), do not play the role of the devil with me by ordering Christ, in me, to accept the kingdoms of the world from you, because I prefer to reject rather than possess them....Finally, accept what the Lord said on this subject, as though it were between me and you: 'Render unto Caesar the things which are Caesar's; and unto God the things that are God's' (Matthew 22:21). And so neither must you surrender what is yours, Caesar, nor must I accept what belongs to Caesar; I shall never accept it even if you offer it thousands of times."

27 What further objections could Constantine have made to this speech by Sylvester, worthy as it is of an apostolic man? Do not those who state that the donation took place insult Constantine, judging, as they do, that he wished to despoil his own family and break apart the Roman Empire? Do they not insult the Senate and People of Rome, Italy, and the whole West, who would have allowed a change in the Empire that went against human and divine law? Would they not be insulting both Sylvester, by alleging he accepted a donation that is unworthy of a holy man, and also the Holy Pontificate, which, they think, was allowed to take possession of earthly kingdoms and to govern the Roman Empire? Yet all this tends to make it evident that, in the midst of so many obstacles, Constantine would never have donated the greater part of the Roman Empire to Sylvester, as those persons claim.

VIII, 28 Now let us proceed. In order to accept as truthful the donation which your document refers to, it must also be established that Sylvester accepted it. Well, this is not evident. But, you state, it is credible that he ratified the donation. I should think so; it is credible that he not only ratified it but also sought it out, demanded it, and extorted it with pleas. But why do you declare as being credible that which is contrary to the opinion of men?...Even if we were to concede that you could produce true documents that are intact and genuine, showing that Sylvester approved, were the donations spoken of in the documents actually granted? Where is the proof that he took possession?...

29 Is it not the case that title was never transferred? It is pure impudence to deny that. Did Constantine ever lead Sylvester triumphantly to the Capitoline hill amidst the applause of the crowds of Romans, even if they were infidels? Did he place him on a golden throne in the presence of the whole Senate? Did he order his officers according to their rank to salute him and worship him as their king?

This is what is usually done with new princes; one does not merely grant them a palace, like the Lateran....Even leaving aside ancient examples, in our memory we have never seen any departure from this practice when someone is made ruler of a city or region or province. Transferral of ownership was recognized only when the former officers were removed and the new ones substituted....Title is not transferred if it remains in the hands of the predecessors and if the new ruler does not dare to remove them....[23]

30 Let us suppose that Sylvester did possess the Empire. Then who took it from him?...If someone does not have ownership and cannot prove that he lost it, surely he never did possess it and, if he says he did, he is mad....Oh, what an astonishing event! The Roman Empire that was created through so much hardship and bloodshed, was both acquired and lost by Christian priests so calmly and quietly, without any bloodshed, war, or conflict! And what is even more amazing, it is altogether unknown by whom, when, or how this was carried out, or how long it lasted. You would think that Sylvester had reigned in sylvan places[24] amid trees, rather than in Rome among men, and that he was driven out by the rains and cold of winter, rather than by men. Whoever has read more than a little, knows how many kings, consuls, dictators, tribunes of the people, censors, and aediles were created in Rome....Yet, even in the city of Rome itself, no one has the slightest knowledge how, when, or by whose efforts the Roman, or Sylvestrian, Empire began or ended. I ask you, what witnesses, what sources can you produce for these events? "None," you reply. Are you not ashamed to say, like beasts

---

[23] "Those things are not regarded as given which do not become the property of the receiver at the moment when they are given." *The Digest of Justinian*, L.xvii.167, trans. Alan Watson (Philadelphia: Univ. of Pennsylvania Press, 1985), 4:967.

[24] Valla is punning on Sylvester's name which has the root *sylva* meaning "forest." The pun may be based on the etymologies of the name Sylvester provided in the life of Saint Sylvester written by Jacobus of Varagine (*The Golden Legend*, ch. 12). The name is said to mean "shady" and to derive from the combination of *silva* ("forest") and *theos* ("God"). See *Legenda aurea*, ed. Th. Graesse (Lipsiae: Librariae Arnoldianae, 1850), 70. The explanation given is different in *The Golden Legend*, trans. and adapted by Granger Ryan and Helmut Ripperger (London, New York, Toronto: Longmans, Green, 1941), 1:72.

rather than men, that it is plausible that Sylvester did possess the Empire?

IX, 31 Since you cannot prove your theory, I shall demonstrate, on the contrary, that Constantine ruled over the Empire until the last day of his life, as did all the other Caesars who followed him. Thus I shall silence you, though you tell me it is a very difficult and laborious task to demonstrate this. Let all the Latin and Greek histories be consulted, let all the other authors who mention that period be cited; you will not find a single discrepancy regarding this matter. Of the thousand testimonies available, one will suffice: Eutropius saw Constantine and his three sons who, at his death, were made rulers over the whole world....[25] This historian would not have kept silent about the donation of the Western Empire had it taken place....

32 At this point I wish to summon all of you recent Roman Pontiffs although you are dead and you, Eugenius, who are living, by the mercy of Pope Felix, however.[26] Why do you proclaim the donation of Constantine so vociferously and, as if you were claimants of the Empire which has been usurped, often threaten certain kings and rulers? Why do you force the emperor and other rulers—the king of Naples and Sicily, for instance—to acknowledge submission at the time of their coronation? None of the early popes of Rome did this....They always recognized that Rome and Italy along with the provinces belonged to the emperors. Furthermore, golden coins exist, not to mention other monuments and temples in Rome, that bear not Greek but Latin inscriptions of Constantine, when he was already a Christian, and of almost all the successive emperors. I own many of these myself....[27] If ever you had ruled over Rome, an infinite number of coins would be found commemorating the

---

[25] The Latin historian of the fourth century, Eutropius, states in his *Breviarium historiae romanae [A Compendium of Roman History]*, that Constantine left his three sons as heirs (X.ix.1).

[26] Pope Eugenius IV (1431–47), the enemy of King Alfonso, was deposed by the Council of Basel in 1439. The antipope elected to replace him was Felix X, who abdicated ten years later when the conciliar movement came to an end. See Ferdinand Gregorovius, *History of the City of Rome in the Middle Ages*, trans. Annie Hamilton (London: George Bell & Sons, 1897), vol. 7, pt. 1, 71–73, 109–10.

[27] Like many other humanists, Valla was interested in numismatics and epigraphy.

Supreme Pontiffs, whereas none are to be found either of gold or silver, and no one remembers having seen any. Yet, at that time, whoever ruled over the Roman Empire would have had to mint his own currency, probably with the image of the Saviour or of Saint Peter....[28]

X, 34 But, so as not to be tedious, it is now time to deal the fatal blow to my adversaries' cause, which has already been beaten and torn to bits, and to slit its throat with a single slash. Almost every history which deserves the name narrates that, right from childhood, Constantine was a Christian (as was his father), and thus a long time before Sylvester became Pope. So writes Eusebius,[29] author of the *Ecclesiastical History*, which Rufinus,[30] a great scholar himself, translated into Latin and to which he added two books on his own times. Both of these writers were virtually contemporaries of Constantine. There is, besides, the testimony of the Roman Pontiff too, who not only participated in these events but actually directed them. He was not merely a witness but also a protagonist who recounts not someone else's but his own actions. I mean Pope Miltiades, Sylvester's immediate predecessor. This is what he writes:

> The Church reached such a stage that not only the peoples of Rome but the rulers too, who held sway over the whole world, flocked to the religion of Christ and to the sacraments of the faith. Among these

---

[28] There is a similar argument, in Prudentius's hymn to Saint Lawrence (vv. 101–4), regarding the absence of coins showing Christ as king, since God, "When He came down to earth below/No coins of Philip [II of Macedon] did He bring,/But without purse, He preached the word/And gave precepts of poverty." *The Poems of Prudentius*, trans. Sister M. Clement Eagan, The Fathers of the Church: A New Translation, vol. 43 (Washington: Catholic Univ. of America Press, 1961), 110.

[29] Eusebius Pamphili, [Bishop of Caesarea]. *Ecclesiastical History*, trans. Roy J. Deferrari, IX.9, The Fathers of the Church: A New Translation, vol. 29 (New York: Fathers of the Church, 1955), 223, describes Constantine thus: "a pious man born of a most pious and in every respect most prudent father." However, in *The Life of Constantine*, trans. E.C. Richardson, chs. 17, 29–32, in *A Select Library of Nicene and Post-Nicene Fathers of the Christian Church*, vol. 1 (Oxford: Parker and Co., 1905), Eusebius speaks of Constantine's conversion late in life. Valla may not have known this work.

[30] Rufinus of Aquileia (d. 410) was an ecclesiastical writer, who wrote an addition to Eusebius's history which ended with the year 324.

Constantine, a most religious man, who was the first to embrace the true faith publicly, not only allowed those who, anywhere in the world, lived within his Empire to become Christians, but he arranged for the building of churches to which he granted lands. And finally the aforementioned ruler contributed immense treasures and began the building of the church which was the first seat of the blessed Peter. He even left his imperial palace and donated it for the benefit of Saint Peter and his successors.[31]

Miltiades states that Constantine gave only the Lateran palace and some land....Where are those who would prevent us from questioning the validity of the donation of Constantine, when that donation occurred before Sylvester's time and involved the transfer of private possessions only?

Although the matter is clear and evident it is still necessary to discuss the text of the privilege itself which those fools commonly cite.[32] **Xl, 35** First of all, one must not only accuse of dishonesty the person who tried to pass himself off as Gratian, and added interpolations in Gratian's work,[33] but one must also accuse of ignorance all those who maintain that the document of the privilege is contained in Gratian—something that learned men have never believed. It is not to be found in the oldest copies of the *Decretum*. And if Gratian had mentioned this event anywhere he would not have mentioned it at the point where they put it, interrupting the flow of the discourse....Some say that the name of the person who added this chapter on the donation was Palea ("Straw"),[34] either

---

[31] Miltiades was pope from 311 to 314. By Valla's time it had been proven that his letter, included in *Decretum*, Part II, *causa* xii, Qu. 1, ch. 15 (see *Patrologia Latina*, ed. J.-P. Migne, vol. 8, col. 566) was apocryphal. Finding it to be useful for his own cause, however, Valla does not hesitate to cite it.

[32] The term privilege refers to the special grant or donation itself, or to the document in which the grant is declared.

[33] The version of the donation analyzed by Valla is slightly different from the one published in the volume of the *Corpus iuris canonici* cited above in note 10.

[34] Palea, an Italian bishop of the 12th century, was a follower and annotator of Gratian. Valla's word play on the name of the author of the interpolations may also suggest that Palea is a man of straw, that is, a screen standing in for another guilty person. In his commentary on Jeremiah 23:28, a verse that contrasts straw and grain, Saint Jerome interprets straw as meaning heretics (see *Patrologia Latina*, vol. 24, cols. 826–27). This meaning was suggested by

because this was actually his name, or else because the things he added, compared to Gratian's, can be likened to straw, or chaff, as opposed to grain. In any case, it is most shameful to believe that the compiler of the *Decretum* was either unaware of such insertions or that he attached great significance to them and considered them true.

Well, that is enough; we have won. First of all because Gratian does not say what those liars have claimed; rather, as a great number of passages indicate, he denies and refutes it. Next, because they cite a single author, one who is unknown and without authority or consequence, and who is, moreover, so stupid as to attribute to Gratian things that could not be reconciled with his other affirmations. Is this, then, the source you are adducing? Are you relying exclusively on this testimony? Do you quote the paltry screed of such an individual in order to verify a matter of such great importance, even though hundreds of categories of proof to the contrary can be enumerated? I was expecting you to show golden seals, marble inscriptions, and a thousand written authorities....

36 ...But just look at how your opinion differs from mine. Even if that privilege had been included in the Life of Sylvester, I do not think it can be taken as true, because that story is not real history, but an imaginary and most impudent fable...and no authority alludes to this privilege. Jacobus da Varagine...in the lives of the saints did not mention the donation of Constantine since it was an imaginary event not worthy of being included among the acts of Sylvester's life.[35] His silence in a certain sense is a judgment against those who are supposed to have recorded it.

37 But it is the forger himself, truly comparable to straw not grain, that I want to take by the neck and drag into court.[36] What are you

---

mediaeval lexicographers too, like Papias who explains that *palea* may be used to indicate sinners.

[35] In *The Golden Legend* (the chapters on Saint Sylvester and the Invention of the Cross) Jacobus da Varagine tells, among other things, of Constantine's conversion, the dream that inspired him to fight the battle of the Mulvian Bridge under Christ's banner, his recovery from leprosy, and his commitment to the building of churches, but says nothing about the donation of the empire.

[36] Cf. Plautus, *Poenulus (The Little Carthaginian)*, III.5.790: "before I'm dragged from here to the judge with my neck in a noose." *Works*, trans. Paul Nixon (Cambridge, MA: Harvard UP and London: William Heinemann, 1980),

saying, you forger? Why is it that we do not read this privilege in the Life of Sylvester?...

But it is foolish of me to attack the audacity of that person rather than the madness of those who have believed it. If someone were to say that it had been handed down among the Greeks, the Jews, or the barbarians, before believing it would you not demand that the author be named, that the manuscript be produced, and that the passage be explained by a faithful interpreter? Now what is being cited is in your language, a well-known manuscript, and either you do not investigate such an incredible deed or, since you can not find the text, you are so credulous that you accept it as having been written down and as being authentic....This donation of Constantine, so magnificent and unprecedented, cannot be proven with any documentation, in gold, silver, bronze or marble or, finally, in book form; rather, if we are to believe these persons, it can be demonstrated only on the basis of paper or parchment....

XII, 38 That madman calls it "the page of the privilege." And you (I wish to attack him as though he were present) call the donation of the whole earth "a privilege"? And you claim that it was written on a "page" and that Constantine used this type of language?...

39 ...You say that...the senate, the optimates, the satraps, as though they were already Christians, together with Caesar decreed to honour the Church of Rome. Why would satraps have taken part? You stupid blockhead![37] Is this how the Caesars speak?...Who has ever heard of satraps being mentioned as members of the councils of the Romans? I do not remember ever having read that anyone in Rome or in the Roman provinces was designated a satrap....

XIV, 44 It is still more absurd and unnatural that Constantinople should be referred to as one of the patriarchal sees, when it was not yet either patriarchal or a see or a Christian city; it was not called Constantinople nor had it yet been founded or even planned. In fact, the privilege was supposedly granted three days after Constantine was converted to Christianity, when it was still Byzantium and not

---

4:79.

[37] Cf. Terence, *Heautontimorumenos* (*The Self-Tormentor*), V.1.877: "Any one of the terms used for a fool...blockhead, wooden-pate...", in *Works*, trans. John Sargeaunt (London: William Heinemann and New York: G.P. Putnam's Sons, 1920), 1:207.

Constantinople....Who fails to see, therefore, that he who drew up the privilege lived a long time after the age of Constantine?...Why does he say "the province of Byzantia"? Byzantium was the name of a city, a place not by any means large enough to accommodate the founding of such a great city. In fact, old Byzantium was enclosed within the walls of Constantinople....

XV, 49 Oh holy Jesus, will you not answer from out of the storm and thunder[38] this man who twists phrases in his uncouth speech? Will you not hurl avenging thunderbolts against such blasphemy? Will you endure such disgrace in your servants? Can you listen to and watch all this and yet close your eyes to it for so long? But "thou...art...longsuffering, and plenteous in mercy" (Psalm 86 [85]:15)....

50 ...Now, let us speak to this deceiver about his crude language. Through his babbling, his shameless forgery reveals itself....Where he deals with the gifts, he says "a diadem...made of pure gold and precious jewels." The ignoramus did not know that the diadem was made of cloth, sometimes silk....He thinks it had to be made of gold, since nowadays kings usually wear a circle of gold set with jewels. But Constantine was not a king and he would never have dared to call himself a king or to adorn himself in regal fashion.[39] He was Emperor of the Romans, not a king....

XVI, 53 The text reads: "Granting him also the imperial sceptres." What a phrase! What elegance! What order! What are these "imperial sceptres"? There is only one sceptre, not several. If indeed an emperor carried a sceptre at all, should the pontiff too bear a sceptre in his hand? Why do we not give him a sword and a helmet and a javelin too?...

XVII, 55 Which should I attack more, the foolishness of the substance or of the words of the privilege?...

---

[38] References to whirlwinds, thunder, and lightning that emanate from God are found in Job 38:1, 41:14 and I Kings 2:10.

[39] Pliny explains that the diadem was "the emblem of royalty" (*Natural History*, VII.57, trans. H. Rackham (London: William Heinemann and Cambridge, MA: Harvard UP, 1942), 635). It was believed that Constantine wore a diadem: see Boninus Mombritius, "Vita Sancti Sylvestri papae et confessoris," *Sanctuarium sive vitae sanctorum* [Milan, c. 1475], ed. A. Brunet and H. Quentin (1910; rpt. Hildesheim-New York: Georg Olms Verlag, 1978), 2:513, l. 26.

XVIII, 58 ...Is the barbarousness of his style not sufficient proof that such a piece of nonsense was forged not in Constantine's day but much later?...

XIX, 62 ...I shall gloss over his reference to..."the province of Byzantia." If you are Constantine, give the reason why you chose that place as the best one for founding the city. In fact, that you move elsewhere after surrendering Rome is not so much "appropriate" as necessary, nor is it right for you to call yourself emperor, since you have lost Rome and have made yourself completely undeserving of the name Roman....

XX, 65 ...Therefore this text is not by Constantine but by some foolish petty cleric who does not know what to say or how to say it. Fat and full, he belches out ideas and words enveloped in fumes of intoxicating wine. But these sentences do not touch others; rather, they turn against the originator himself....

XXII, 69 [The text ends with the words] "Dated at Rome, the third day before the Kalends of April, in the fourth consulate of Constantine Augustus..." The word "dated" [Latin *datum* ("given")] is used only in letters and nowhere else, except by the ignorant. For letters are given to the addressees or to the courier who brings them to the addressees....But since the so-called privilege of Constantine was not to be delivered to anyone, one should not have said it was "given." Thus it is plain to see that the person who wrote this was lying and was unable to feign what Constantine would have probably said and done.

70 The stupidity and folly of the forger are shared equally by those who believe that he told the truth and who defend it, although they now have no arguments to defend or even honestly justify their opinion. Or can it be an honest excuse for an error when you see truth revealed and refuse to accept it, just because certain great persons thought differently? These persons were great, I dare say, only because of their office, not for their knowledge or ability. And yet how do you know that those whose belief you subscribe to, if they had heard the arguments you have heard, would have remained in their opinion, or would they perhaps have changed their minds? And yet it is most shameful to wish to defer to a human being rather than to truth, that is God.[40] Certain individuals who are bereft of arguments usually

---

[40] "Jesus saith unto him, I am the way, the truth, and the life" (John 14:6).

answer me this way: "Then why have so many holy pontiffs believed that the donation was true?" I call you as witnesses, you are leading me where I do not wish to go, and you are urging me, against my will, to speak ill of the Supreme Pontiffs, whose misdeeds I should rather conceal.

But let us go on speaking frankly, since this case cannot be handled in any other way. **XXIII, 71** I admit that they believed this and that they did not act maliciously. What is strange about their having believed these things, which are appealing because they involve great profit, when, out of remarkable ignorance, they believe many superstitious things in which there is no apparent profit?...

XXV, 80 But, you say, "why is it that the emperors who suffered a loss because of the donation of Constantine, do not deny it, but rather recognize, proclaim and maintain it?"...

83 ...Whoever calls himself Emperor of the Romans, in my opinion, is neither Augustus nor Caesar nor emperor, unless he holds power over Rome, and, if he does not try to recover the city of Rome, he is clearly a perjurer. The former Caesars, beginning with Constantine, were not forced to take the oath that is demanded of the Caesars now. They were required, as far as humanly possible, not to decrease the expanse of the Roman Empire in the least; rather they were to seek diligently to enlarge it....The Supreme Pontiff might more correctly be called Augustus from the word *augere* ("to increase"),[41] except that while he increases his temporal power, he diminishes his spiritual one. And so you observe that the worst among the Supreme Pontiffs tried hardest to defend the donation, for example, Boniface VIII, who deceived Celestinus with the pipes inserted in the wall.[42] He wrote about the donation of

---

[41] Valla actually rejects the belief, held by many, including Isidore of Seville (*Etymologies*, IX.iii.16) that the name Augustus refers to the tendency to enlarge the republic. In his discussion Valla stresses the derivation of *Augustus* from *ab avium gustu* ("from the way birds eat"), a phrase that, according to the explication given by Suetonius (*The Deified Augustus*, 7) among others, refers to consecration through augural rites. The two etymologies referring to augmenting and augury are connected, in the sense that an augur was someone who foretold that an undertaking would flourish. See A. Ernout and A. Meillet, *Dictionnaire étymologique de la langue latine: Histoire des mots* (Paris: Librairie C. Klincksieck, 1959), 57.

[42] According to legend, Pope Boniface VIII (1295–1303) deceived his

Constantine and stripped the king of France and, as though wishing to put the donation of Constantine into practice, he established that the kingdom itself belonged to and was subject to the Church of Rome.[43] This is something that his successors Benedict and Clement immediately revoked as being dishonest and unjust.

But, oh Roman Pontiffs, what is the meaning of this concern of yours to demand that the donation of Constantine be confirmed by every single emperor, if not that you are unsure of your own legal right? But your argument backfires, as one says, since that donation never existed, and "that which does not exist can not be confirmed"[44] and, whatever the Caesars donate, they donate having been deceived by Constantine's example, and they have no right to donate the Empire.

XXVI, 84 Now let us suppose that Constantine made the donation and that Sylvester acquired possession at one time but that later either he or one of his successors was stripped of it....I say that neither according to divine law nor human law may you legally proceed to sue for recovery.[45] In the Old Testament a Jew was forbidden to serve another Jew for more than six years[46] and after

---

predecessor Celestinus V, forcing him to abdicate after a few months. "It is said that in the silence of the night [he], by means of a speaking tube, summoned him as by a voice from heaven to renounce the Papacy, and that this stratagem moved the tortured man to a step hitherto unknown in the annals of the Church" (Gregorovius, V.2.525).

[43] The struggle between the pope and the French king Philip the Fair (1285–1314), who resisted ecclesiastical supremacy, is described by Gregorovius (570–72). Boniface's ban excommunicating the king was lifted by his more accommodating successors Benedict XI (1303–4) and Clement V (1305–14).

[44] This is one of the maxims in the *Rule of Law* dealing with the act of confirming. See *Regulae iuris*, ed. F. Frommelt (Lipsiae: Weiss and Neumeister, 1880), 25.

[45] Valla uses the legal term *recuperatio*, which is explained by Berger as follows: "A treaty between Rome and another state under which reciprocal protection of the citizens of one state in the territory of the other was established, in particular in case of litigation for the recovery of property" (669).

[46] "And if thy brother, an Hebrew man, or an Hebrew woman, be sold unto thee, and serve thee six years; then in the seventh year thou shalt let him go free from thee" (Deuteronomy 15:12).

fifty years everything reverted to the original owner.[47] Can it be that in the era of grace a Christian may be condemned to eternal slavery by the vicar of Christ, who redeemed us from servitude? Or rather, will he be returned to slavery after having been freed and having enjoyed freedom for a long time?

85 I shall pass over in silence how ferocious, violent, and cruel the rule of priests often is....And will we not be allowed to rebel against such a great tyranny? And especially against those who,...from being shepherds of the flock, that is of souls, have become thieves and bandits.

XXVII, 86 As far as human law is concerned, who is ignorant of the fact that war does not confer any right or, if it does, the title is valid only as long as you possess what you have acquired through war? Since, when you lose ownership, you lose title as well. And so, if prisoners of war flee, no one prosecutes them[48] and, similarly, booty is not reclaimed if the original owners recover it.... **87** ...The Romans declared war against others for the same reason that other peoples and kings did, and those who were attacked and defeated in war had the right to rebel against the Romans, just as they rebelled against other masters, unless (and no one would say this) all regimes should be brought back to the most ancient and very first holders, that is to those who first seized what belonged to others....

88 ...And, if it is legitimate for the nations under Rome to elect a king or to set up a republic, all the more will it be legitimate for the Roman people to do so, especially in light of the new tyranny of the pope.

XXVIII, 89 Unable to defend the donation (because it never existed and, if it had, because of the time that has elapsed, it would now be invalid), our adversaries take refuge in another type of defence....They say that the Church of Rome obtained its possessions through prescription.[49] ...Then why is the Church so concerned with having the emperors confirm its title? Why does it

---

[47] "And ye shall hallow the fiftieth year, and proclaim liberty throughout all the land...and ye shall return every man unto his possession, and ye shall return every man unto his family" (Leviticus 25:10).

[48] "Freemen are reduced to slavery but those who escape the power of the enemy regain their original freedom" (*The Digest*, XLI.i.7 [7:488]).

[49] See note 12 above on prescription.

proclaim the donation and the Caesars' confirmation of it, if one of the two is sufficient?...

"The Church of Rome gained possession through prescription." And how can it have carried out this prescription, when possession is based not on a legitimate title[50] but on bad faith?[51] Or, if you deny that it is a possession in bad faith, you certainly cannot deny that it is based on a groundless faith? Or, in such an important and obvious matter, should one excuse ignorance of the facts and of the law?[52] Of the facts, precisely because Constantine did not surrender Rome and the provinces (a fact that may elude the common man, but not the Supreme Pontiff); ignorance of the law also, because those provinces could not be either donated or accepted—something that no Christian should be ignorant of....But if you still continue to have possession, then ignorance has been transformed into malice and fraud, and clearly you have become a possessor in bad faith.[53]

90 "The Church of Rome gained possession through prescription." Oh you incompetents, ignorant of divine law! No number of years, no matter how great, can cancel a real title. Indeed, if I were captured by barbarians and believed dead, once I return to the fatherland after one hundred years of captivity, would I be prevented from reclaiming my father's inheritance?[54] What could be more inhuman?...

"The Church of Rome gained possession through prescription." Be silent, evil tongue! You are applying the type of prescription that concerns inanimate and irrational things to man, whose enslavery is all the more detestable, the longer it lasts. Birds and beasts do not submit to prescription; rather, no matter how long the period of captivity lasts, when it pleases them and when the opportunity arises, they flee. And is it not legitimate for a man held by another

---

[50] "The law forbids possessors to demand ownership, if they did not obtain possession by a good title" (*The Code*, III.xxxii.24 [6:316]).

[51] According to a maxim of the *Rule of Law* regarding possession in good and bad faith, he who possesses in bad faith is not allowed to avail himself of prescription (55). See Berger (638), on "Possessor bonae fidei."

[52] *The Digest* (XXII.vi) deals with ignorance of the law and of the facts.

[53] One of the *Laws of the Twelve Tables* of the Romans (III.1) demands double compensation from someone who took possession fraudulently. See *The Civil Law* (New York: AMS Press, 1973), 1:62.

[54] The question is discussed in *The Digest*, XLIX.xv.19.

man to flee? **91** ...A short time before I was born (and I call to witness the memory of those who were present), Rome, although she had been free for a long time, was subjected, through an extraordinary type of fraud, to papal rule or, rather, papal tyranny. The pope in question was Boniface IX, equal to the eighth in evildoing as well as in name,[55] if, that is, those who do great evil may call themselves Boniface ("doer of good"). When, after the deceit was discovered, the Romans became indignant, the good pope, following Tarquin's example, struck the "tallest poppies" with his rod.[56] When later his successor Innocent tried to imitate him, he was driven out of the city.[57] I do not wish to speak of the other popes, who always kept Rome oppressed by force, although she rebelled whenever she could, as, for example, six years ago. When Rome was unable to obtain peace from Eugenius or face the enemies that were besieging her, she herself besieged the pope in his palace and did not allow him to leave until he made peace with the enemies or handed the administration of the city over to the citizens. But he preferred to leave the city in disguise with a single companion in his flight, rather than satisfy the citizens' just and fair requests.[58] If you give them a choice, who fails to see that they would choose freedom over slavery?... **93** Supreme Pontiff, we have come of our own free will to you so that you might rule over us; now of our own free will we are distancing ourselves from you, so that you will not rule over us any longer. If we are in some way indebted to you, let

---

[55] Boniface IX (1389–1404) astutely succeeded in making a treaty with the Romans whereby he could become master of the city. Thus he brought about the downfall of the Roman republic and subdued the rebellious conspirators. These events are told in Gregorovius, VI.2.544–53.

[56] Livy (I.liv.6–8 [1:189]) narrates that Tarquin struck off the heads off the "tallest poppies" with his stick, to suggest to his son that the chief men of the state should be eliminated.

[57] Innocent VII (1404–6) was forced to flee from Rome for a brief period in 1405 when his nephew massacred the people's envoys. See Gregorovius, VI.2.576–78.

[58] The Romans rebelled against Pope Eugenius on May 29, 1434 and demanded their freedom. He was forced to flee disguising himself as a Benedictine, taking refuge in Florence, where, joined by the members of the Curia, he stayed until September 1443. He was still in exile when Valla wrote his treatise on the donation. On these events see Gregorovius, VII.1.44–47, 88.

us calculate our debts and credits. But you wish to rule over us against our will, as though we were underlings, we who perhaps could govern more wisely than you....The people called you here, Supreme Pontiff, as a father or, if you please, as a lord, not as an enemy or an executioner. But you do not wish to act as a father or lord, but as an enemy and executioner. And yet, since we are Christians, we shall not imitate your cruelty and evil, even if we could by the law of reprisal, nor shall we brandish a vengeful sword over your head; rather, after forcing you to resign and sending you away, we shall adopt another father or lord....

XXIX, 94 But what need is there to say more about such an obvious matter? I maintain that not only did Constantine not confer so many grants, not only was the Roman Pontiff not able to win them by means of prescription, but even if both did occur, yet both titles would have been annulled because of the misdeeds of the title-holders, when we consider that the ruin and devastation of the whole of Italy and many provinces have stemmed from this single source....

XXX, 97 And so nowhere is there any religion, any sanctity, any fear of God, and (I hate to mention it even) evil men find in the pope an excuse for all their crimes....

98 Thus, can we believe that God would have allowed Sylvester to accept opportunities for sin? I will not allow this insult to be brought against a most holy man, or this offence to be made against an excellent pontiff, that it can be said that he accepted empires, kingdoms, and provinces, things which are renounced even by those who want to become mere priests. Sylvester possessed little, as did the other holy popes....But the Supreme Pontiffs of our time, who abound in wealth and pleasure, strive, it appears, to be wicked and foolish (just as much as the early popes strove to be wise and holy), and to outdo with every kind of infamy the brilliant glory of their predecessors. Can anyone who deserves to be called a Christian tolerate this calmly?

99 Even so, in this first oration of mine, I do not wish to exhort rulers and peoples to restrain the pope as he hastens on his unbridled course and force him to remain within his own territory, but simply to warn him. Perhaps he is already conscious of this and will leave other people's lands and of his own will make his way to his own home; abandoning the furious waves and violent storms, he will return into port. If he refuses to do so, then I shall set about writing another much more ferocious discourse.[59] Oh, how I hope (and there is nothing that I desire more, especially if it comes about through my advice) that one day the pope will be the vicar of Christ only and not also of Caesar. No longer will one hear those terrible words: "supporters of the Church" or "opponents of the Church"....It is the pope, not the Church, who is warring against Christians. The Church, instead, fights only "against spiritual wickedness in high places" (Paul, Ephesians 6:12). Then the pope will be deemed (and will truly be) a holy father, the father of all, the father of the Church. He will not stir up wars among Christians; on the contrary, if they are initiated by others, he will terminate them with his apostolic censure and papal majesty.

[59] Valla did not write a second discourse on the subject.

Publications of the
Centre for Reformation and Renaissance Studies

Renaissance and Reformation Texts in Translation:

Jean Bodin. *On the Demon-Mania of Witches.* Abridged, trans. & ed. R.A. Scott and J.L. Pearl. 218 pp.

Nicholas of Cusa. *The Layman on Wisdom and The Mind.* Trans. & ed. M.L. Führer. 111 pp.

Giovanni Della Casa. *Galateo: A Renaissance Treatise on Manners.* 3rd ed. rev. Trans. & ed. K. Eisenbichler and K.R. Bartlett. 100 pp.

Andreas Karlstadt, Hieronymous Emser, Johannes Eck. *A Reformation Debate: Karlstadt, Emser, and Eck on Sacred Images.* Trans. & ed. Bryan Mangrum and Giuseppe Scavizzi. 2nd ed. rev. 125 pp.

Bernardino Ochino. *Seven Dialogues.* Trans. & ed. R. Belladonna. xlviii, 96 pp.

Lorenzo Valla. *'The Profession of the Religious' and 'The Falsely-Believed and Forged Donation of Constantine'.* 3rd ed. rev. Trans. & ed. Olga Z. Pugliese. 114 pp.

Whether Secular Government Has the Right to Wield the Sword in Matters of Faith. A Controversy in Nürnberg in 1530. Trans. & ed. J. Estes. 118 pp.

Tudor and Stuart Texts:

James I. *The True Law of Free Monarchies and Basilikon Doron.* Ed. with an intro. by D. Fischlin and M. Fortier. 181 pp.

The Trial of Nicholas Throckmorton. Ed. with an intro. by Annabel Patterson. 108 pp.

Early Stuart Pastoral. The Shepherd's Pipe *by George Wither and Others,* and The Shepherd's Hunting *by George Wither.* Ed. with an intro. by J. Doelman. Forthcoming (January 1999).

Occasional Publications:

Jacqueline Glomski and Erika Rummel. *Early Editions of Erasmus at the Centre for Reformation and Renaissance Studies, Toronto.* 153 pp.

Millar MacLure. *Register of Sermons Preached at Paul's Cross 1534-1642.* Rev. P. Pauls and J.C. Boswell. 152 pp.